CROWN
OF A
THOUSAND
YEARS

CROWN OF A THOUSAND YEARS

A Millennium of British History
presented as a pageant of
Kings and Queens

by M. E. Hudson and Mary Clark

11934

CROWN PUBLISHERS, INC., NEW YORK

First published in 1947 by Harper of Holloway
Revised and enlarged edition designed, produced
and published in 1978 by Alphabet and Image, Sherborne, Dorset, England.

First published in the U.S.A. by Crown Publishers, Inc., 1978

Acknowledgments

The sources of illustrations are given beneath the reproductions. Acknowledgment is made to His Grace the
Archbishop of Canterbury and the Trustees of Lambeth Palace Library, the Trustees of the British Museum, the
National Portrait Gallery, and The Royal Academy for access to the works of art and permission to reproduce them granted
to the copyright holder Frank Harper in respect of all photographs taken by E. D. Blann. These comprise all the
illustrations with the exception of those on page 9 (courtesy the Trustees of the British Museum), page 48 (courtesy the Chapter
of Gloucester Cathedral), page 53, page 58 (courtesy the Dean and Chapter of Canterbury Cathedral) and page 149 (courtesy the Worshipful
Company of Fishmongers, Pietro Annigoni and Arts Unlimited, London and Rugby), which were taken by Michael Holford; on
page 2 (courtesy the Chapter Trustees, Kings Lynn) which was taken by P. M. Goodchild; on page 79, which was provided by
The Walker Art Gallery, Liverpool; on page 144, which was provided by courtesy of Lord Brownlow; on page 145, by courtesy
of Angus District Council; and those pictures on pages 59, 84, 107, 119 and 127
which were provided by The National Portrait Gallery.

The picture on page 2 shows King John's Cup, Kings Lynn.

Library of Congress Cataloging in Publication Data

Hudson, Mildred, 1902–1961.
  Crown of a thousand years.

  1. Great Britain—Kings and rulers—Biography.
2. Great Britain—Kings and rulers—Portraits.
I. Clarke, Mary, 1944–   joint author.
II. Title.
DA28.1.H83   1978   941'.00992   78-4466
ISBN 0-517-53452-5

Filmset by Keyspools Ltd, Golborne, Warrington
Printed in Great Britain by Sackville Press Billericay Ltd, Essex
and bound by Webb Son & Co. Ltd, Ferndale, Glamorgan

Contents

Prelude

'Britain,' wrote the Venerable Bede in 731, 'is an island in the Ocean,' and in this lies the country's strength and weakness. The seas have brought many different men and customs and languages to Britain since the days before history began, and history began in about 332 BC when Pytheas, a merchant from Marseilles, made a voyage of discovery along the Atlantic coast, and wrote about his visit to Britain. The next major historical record is Julius Caesar's narrative of his landing in Kent in 55 BC. The Roman conquest of Britain began in earnest under the Emperor Claudius in AD 43, and the Celtic natives, their tribal system, their individual style of pottery and jewellery, their coinage and their trade were swamped by the Roman way of life. But the Romans brought their brilliant engineering techniques, the Latin language and, later, Christianity.

In the fourth century Britain shared in the decline and fall of the Roman Empire and was subject to constant raids from barbarians from Northern Europe. In the early fifth century a chronicler from Gaul wrote, 'the Britons in these days by all kinds of calamities and disasters are falling into the power of the Saxons.' The British monk Gildas, writing one hundred years later, quotes a letter sent to Rome at this time calling for help: 'To Aetius, three times Consul, the groans of the Britons: the barbarians drive us to the sea, the sea drives us to the barbarians: between these two methods of death we are either massacred or drowned.' To these shadowy times belongs the story of a great leader who gathered a group of Romano-British followers and fought the barbarians to the death. This was the legendary but shadowy King Arthur and his Knights of the Round Table.

In his *Ecclesiastical History of the English Nation* the chronicler Bede describes the barbarians who came and settled in Britain – the Jutes, the Angles and the Saxons. Organized Christianity in Britain collapsed or withdrew to isolated parts of Wales and Ireland. In AD 596 Pope Gregory sent St Augustine and a group of monks to England. Bede writes that they 'were appalled at the idea of going to a barbarous, fierce and pagan nation', but they found that once they had converted the rulers, the people were ready to abandon their old gods and accept a new one, and by the seventh century there was a remarkable flowering of literature and learning in the churches and monasteries of Britain. By this period the seven kingdoms of Northumbria, Mercia, Wessex, East Anglia, Essex, Kent and Sussex had emerged from the political relics of Roman Britain. But the fabric of Anglo-Saxon society was itself threatened by the Danish raids which began in the late eighth century. The Danes came over the seas in longboats first to plunder, then to settle. The exertions of Alfred the Great, King of Wessex in the ninth century, restricted the Danish invaders to eastern and northern parts of Britain which became known as the Danelaw. It was Alfred who paved the way for the kings of the House of Wessex to dominate and subdue the country. By AD 937 Athelstan of Wessex was able to describe himself as 'most glorious King of the Anglo-Saxons and Danes'. Nearly forty years later in 973, his nephew Edgar was crowned at Bath in a spectacular ceremony on which all English coronation orders have since been based. But Edgar died two years later at the age of thirty-three, leaving no strong successor. His sons Edward and Ethelred, both by different mothers and both under age, were backed by different and opposing rival factions. The elder, Edward, became King but was murdered three years later at Corfe in Dorset on a visit to his step-mother. He was buried at Wareham.

Ethelred 978–1016

Ethelred was about twelve years old in 978 when his half-brother was killed. Although he was not responsible for the assassination, it marked a bad beginning to a reign that worsened as it went on. Ethelred came to be known as 'Unready', from the old English word *redeless* meaning ill-counselled, because he was unable to distinguish between good advice and bad. Although his predecessor Edward has been described by one historian as a youth of 'intolerable violence in speech and behaviour', his supporters re-buried his body in state in Shaftesbury and were soon claiming that miracles occurred through his intercession. Thirty years after Edward's death, the harassed Ethelred was forced to proclaim 18 March as the festival of Saint Edward 'the Martyr'.

The year after Ethelred became King, the Danish raids on England began again, and during the next thirty-eight years the invaders steadily gained ground despite the King's policy of buying off the enemy with huge sums of money known as Danegeld. The *Anglo-Saxon Chronicle* speaks scathingly of the feeble defence put up by Ethelred, but one of the King's most brutal and ill-advised acts was to order a massacre of all the Danes living in England in November, 1002, as reported by the thirteenth-century chronicler John of Wallingford: 'The English agreed together that each province should kill the Danes at that time resident within its limits, and they appointed a certain day on which they should rise against them. They spared neither sex nor age, destroying together with them those women of their own nation who had consented to intermix with the Danes, and the children who had sprung from that foul adultery. Some women had their breasts cut off, others were buried alive in the ground, and the children were dashed to pieces against posts, stones. . . . Twelve young men who escaped set off for Denmark. With weeping and mourning did they tell Swein their King what had been done in England, and immediately he, burning to be revenged, summoned his Counsel.' The terrible series of punitive raids which followed culminated in 1013, when Swein Forkbeard landed in England at Sandwich, and Ethelred fled for refuge to the Duke of Normandy whose sister, Emma, he had married. Swein was left master of England, but died a few months later at Gainsborough. Although the Danelaw accepted his twenty-year old son Canute as King, the West Saxon Witan, an assembly of wise men, recalled Ethelred, declaring that 'no lord was dearer to them than their natural lord, if he would but rule them better than he had before.' Ethelred returned and spent two miserable years fighting ill-health and Canute. He died in London in April 1016.

Canute 1017–1035

Ethelred's son, Edmund Ironside, fought on heroically against Canute, but died the same year as his father, and in the absence of any able British successor the Witan accepted Canute as King of England. Canute's father, Swein Forkbeard, had been converted to Christianity in his later years, and it was as a Christian king that Canute ascended the throne of England in 1017, marking the conquest of England by the Danes.

Silver coins   *British Museum*

Ethelred
Harold Harefoot

Canute
Harthacanute

Canute proved to be one of the ablest kings in Northern Europe. As well as England, he ruled Denmark and Norway and was the acknowledged over-lord of Ireland, Scotland and Wales. One of his first actions as King was to send for Ethelred's widow, Emma, whom he married on condition that any children either of them had produced up to that date should be disinherited. Canute brought peace and law and order to the exhausted country. He firmly consolidated his position with the backing of his standing army, or huscarles, his efficient fleet and his great law code of 1020 which reflected his acceptance of the existing legal systems. He divided the country into earldoms, and founded many churches and shrines for which he was highly praised by the monastic chroniclers. But he is best known for an act that is sadly distorted by popular history. He did not try to turn back the waves to show his power, but endured his wetting to teach his courtiers the wisdom of Christian humility, and to worship the Creator of the tides, and not a mere king.

Canute died at Shaftesbury in November 1035, aged about forty, and was buried at Winchester. He left several possible heirs, although he had intended Harthacanute, his son by Emma of Normandy, to succeed him.

Harold Harefoot and Harthacanute
1035–1042

Harthacanute was in Denmark when his father died, and his disinherited and illegitimate half-brother, Harold Harefoot, seized the throne. The following year, Alfred and Edward, Emma's sons by Ethelred, arrived in England to visit their mother at Winchester. Alfred was captured, tortured and killed by Godwin, Earl of Wessex, one of Harold's supporters. Edward fled back to Normandy and Emma was expelled from England. Harold lived only another four years, until March 1039, and Harthacanute arrived back in England to claim the throne. He had Harold's body exhumed and thrown into the Thames, oppressed his subjects with the severity of his taxation and died suddenly in 1042, 'as he stood at his drink'. The Witan rejected the next Danish candidate for the crown, Canute's nephew Swein, and elected Etheldred's son Edward as King. Once again a prince of the House of Wessex sat on the throne of England.

Edward the Confessor 1042–1066

Edward the Confessor is something of an enigma. Later legend has painted the picture of a frail, monk-like figure with long white hair and a dignified bearing. A saintly man but a weak king. Yet some contemporaries talk of his violent temper, his love of hunting and his harsh treatment of his mother, Emma, for favouring her sons by Canute over her sons by Ethelred. Wherever the truth lies it is certain that the middle-aged man who succeeded the sons of Canute came to England as much a foreigner as they were. Although born at Islip near Oxford, he had spent most of his life in Normandy, a wealthy and sophisticated state in comparison with Anglo-Saxon England. Not unnaturally, Edward's manners, speech, tastes and closest companions were Norman. When high positions of Church and state were given to Normans, the English earls objected. The leader of the nationalistic party was Godwin, Earl of Wessex, who in 1036 had caused the death of Edward's brother Alfred. Edward owed his accession to Godwin's backing, and he married the Earl's daughter Edith in 1045, though it was said that the marriage was never consummated.

The growing power of Godwin's family was in turn resented as much by the old northern earls as it was by the King's Norman advisers. Men such as Robert of Jumièges, the newly-appointed Archbishop of Canterbury, and Siward, the long-established Earl of Northumbria, were eager to create trouble between Godwin and the King. Their chance came in the summer of 1051 when Godwin defied the King over an incident concerning one of Edward's Norman relatives. Godwin could find no support from the peers and was forced to flee into exile. For a time the Normans reigned supreme at court, and it could have been at this time that William of Normandy visited England and extracted a promise from Edward that he should be his heir. This is what William was later to insist, but there is no historical record of the event. Edward's subjects came to dislike the influence of the Normans at court even more than that of

11

Manuscript   *British Museum*

Edward the Confessor

Godwin, and thus Edward, who had apparently reduced the armed strength of his kingdom, was unable to prevent Godwin's return in 1052, and was forced to reinstate his overmighty subject. Godwin died seven months later at a great feast in Winchester, and his eldest surviving son, Harold, succeeded his father as the power behind, if not before, the throne.

Edward became increasingly pious as he got older, and devoted many of the remaining years of his life to the building of an abbey church at Westminster, to be larger and grander than any church in England or Normandy, and to be modelled on the Norman Abbey at Jumièges. Norman craftsmen spent fifteen years building the great church on the marshy land by the River Thames. Next to the Abbey, Edward built himself a palace where it seems no one had a room to himself except the King, and the Treasury consisted of a large chest kept under Edward's bed. On 28 December 1065 the Abbey of Westminster was consecrated. Edward was too ill to attend the ceremony and died eight days later, on 5 January 1066, nominating Godwin's son Harold, Earl of Wessex, as his successor.

Edward's death is vividly depicted in the Bayeux tapestry, with Edward's weeping Queen at the foot of the bed, and the royal body being shrouded for burial. The next scene shows the open bier being carried to the Abbey, escorted by a prelate and attendant priests. The newness of the Abbey is symbolized by a man climbing to place the weathercock in position. Edward was buried behind the high altar of the Abbey and his shrine quickly became a favourite spot for devotions and alleged miracles. A century later Edward was canonized and remained England's favourite saint until he was superseded by St George in the fourteenth century.

Harold 1066

Harold Godwinson had no claim to the throne of England other than Edward's recommendation and a conviction that he had earned it. Hereditary succession was by no means yet the rule, and as the late King's court was clearly prepared to accept Harold, he was crowned with great solemnity in Westminster Abbey on the same day that Edward was buried. But Harold laboured under various disadvantages. He had earlier alienated his younger brother Tostig, who had gone to Norway to intrigue with King Harold Hardrada. The Norwegian king felt he had a claim to the English throne as a descendant of King Canute.

More immediately, Harold had upset Duke William of Normandy, who claimed that Edward had promised the throne to him. What was worse, William accused Harold of being an oath-breaker, a serious sin in the eyes of the Church and a crime in the eyes of the state. About two years before the Confessor died, Harold had been wrecked off the coast of France while on a pleasure trip up the channel. Edward's kinsman, William of Normandy, had entertained Harold with lavish hospitality but had declined to allow him to return home until he had sworn to support William's claim to the English throne when Edward died. Harold later claimed that he had been tricked into swearing the oath on a formidable collection of religious relics. However, the Pope in Rome was only too willing to support William's cry of 'perjured usurper', as he had been involved in a long-standing dispute with Stigand, Archbishop of Canterbury. To these forces mounted against Harold seems to have been added the wrath of God, for not long after his accession 'a hairy star was seen, not only in England, but – or so they say – throughout the entire world, shining for seven days with great brightness.' The men of 1066 were not to know that this was Halley's comet. They took it as a portent of disaster.

In spite of the powerful position he had held for so long in England, Harold had done little to improve the cumbersome machinery of government or the out-of-date military organization. In the first few weeks of his reign, he threw himself into the task of gathering a fleet and an army. He deployed his country levies along the south coast, and his fleet off the Isle of Wight, and waited for William to arrive. But the summer passed uneventfully and Harold's fighting force had to disband in early September to gather in the harvest, while the fleet moved up into the Thames estuary. The north winds that kept William in Normandy helped Tostig and Harold Hardrada to reach the Yorkshire coast where they defeated levies of troops and encamped near York at Stamford Bridge. With his Danish household troops, the huscarles, Harold sped north and in a spectacular and hard-fought battle won one of the most complete victories of the Middle Ages. Heaps of bones marked the site of the battle for over seventy years. But at the moment of triumph, Harold heard the news that William of Normandy had landed at Pevensey in Sussex on 29 September.

Always inclined to be impetuous and over-confident, Harold decided to force a battle. Within five days he was back in London recalling his army. In another five days he was marching south to meet William near Hastings, and took up his position on Senlac Hill, just outside the town. Although the Normans were a better-equipped and trained fighting force, the wood and marsh which flanked Harold's site made it difficult for William to use his cavalry to the best advantage. Harold's huscarles formed an almost impenetrable wall with their interlocked shields, and after fighting in vain for six hours, William finally broke through by a deliberately feigned flight. The unsuspecting Saxons broke ranks, pursued the Normans and lost their advantage. Harold and his huscarles fought on until evening, broken at the end by the pitiless rain of Norman arrows. Tradition has it that Harold was hit in the eye and his household troops stayed and died to a man around him. William's chaplain, William of Poitiers, wrote of the end: 'In the English ranks the only movement was the dropping of the dead; the living stood motionless.' Thus passed the last king of Saxon England. His body was buried in the cliffs above the sea-shore but was eventually transferred to Waltham Abbey, a church Harold himself had founded.

Bayeux Tapestry

Harold

16

Bayeux Tapestry

William I

17

William I 1066-1087

William I was the illegitimate son of Duke Robert of Normandy and Arlette, a tanner's daughter from Falaise. His father died when he was seven and William had a long hard struggle to secure his inheritance. This made him a good soldier but a hard man, although he had a reputation for being just and clean-living. After the battle of Hastings, William made his way to London, laying waste the countryside around the city, which quickly submitted to him. He was crowned on Christmas Day in Westminster Abbey by Aldred, Archbishop of York, using the traditional Anglo-Saxon coronation ceremony.

It took the new King five years to subdue the country and crush rebellions, and to those who opposed him and planned revolt William could be ruthlessly severe. The north became the last stronghold of the Saxon earls and was the centre of frequent disturbances. William marched north in 1070, cowed the city of York, and harried the county of Yorkshire with such deliberate savagery that the whole country was blackened and depopulated for over a century. The last serious revolt against the Normans was in 1071 in the Fens, where a Lincolnshire man, known as Hereward the Wake, led a group of outlaws who became famous for their defiance of William. They were eventually crushed, although Hereward himself escaped, and William admitted that 'if there had been three Herewards in England, I should not have conquered the country.'

The hard-headed and tenacious Normans were of Viking stock who had assumed the religion and customs of France. William, a fine example of his race, was not only an intrepid soldier but also a great administrator, with an eye for the details of government and a sound political instinct. He was only too well aware of the dangers inherent in the old Anglo-Saxon earldoms, and therefore redistributed the land according to the law of Norman feudalism. By this system the King owned the land but leased it out to his nobles or tenants-in-chief, who in their turn sub-let to their knights, and so on down the social hierarchy. Thus each land holder owed military service, feudal dues and personal allegiance to his over-lord: 'everybody had to belong to somebody else and everybody else to the King', as the authors of *1066 and All That* so aptly put it. William also scattered the land holdings of his most powerful nobles in different parts of the country, making it almost impossible for any one man to gather his forces in sufficient strength to trouble the King without the fact being known. The Anglo-Saxon tradition of local self-government was largely retained, for the Normans were a minority group and could not afford to alienate the mass of the people by sweeping aside their well-established customs and traditions.

In order to record the rights of the crown, William the Conqueror ordered the compiling of the Domesday Book, so called because, as a contemporary explained, 'it spared no man but judged all men indifferently, as the Lord in the great day will do.' The Domesday Book, which took six years to complete, is a unique and monumental survey, unequalled in comprehensiveness and detail until the nineteenth century, of all the land holdings in the country, their size, proprietors, tenures, value, the proportion of meadow, pasture, wood and arable land, and sometimes the number of tenants, cottagers, free and un-free men. The chief purpose of the survey was financial, to create some machinery which should make the assessment and collection of feudal rents easier. In 1086, when the Domesday Book was finished, William summoned 'all the land-holding men of any account throughout England, whosoever men they were', to a great meeting at Salisbury, where they all took an oath of allegiance to the King.

William was a devoted son of the Church. His appointments were unpopular with the English bishops because it was his policy always to fill empty places with Normans. However, his appointees were generally men of learning and good character, the most outstanding among them being Lanfranc, whom William called from St Stephen's Abbey at Caen to be Primate. The Norman bishops tightened up discipline among the English clergy and brought the English Church into closer contact with the Church in Europe. William gave his personal encouragement to the Norman bishops in the building of their great cathedrals and abbeys, such as St Albans, Tewkesbury and Exeter; their monumental Romanesque architecture, known in England as 'Norman', setting a tradition which was to last for more than a century.

Even after his conquest of England, William's main interest and concern was his Duchy of Normandy, where he was constantly involved in border disputes with his over-lord, the King of France. After the great meeting at Salisbury in 1086, William returned to Normandy, and saw England for the last time. In an attack on the French town of Mantes the following year, his horse reared, causing him internal injuries, and the King was carried to Rouen to die. William's wife, Matilda of Flanders, to whom he had been devoted, had died in 1085 leaving five daughters and three sons, Robert, William and Henry, who were called to their father's deathbed. William died on 9 September, commending his soul to God, the Duchy of Normandy to Robert, the crown of England to William and £5,000 to Henry. He was buried in his favourite abbey, St Stephen at Caen. *The Anglo-Saxon Chronicle* says of the old King, 'He was a very wise and great man, more honoured and more powerful than any before him. Amongst other things, the good peace that he made in the land must not be forgotten.'

William II 1087–1100

In theory William II should never have been King. Having emphasized the law of primogeniture in England, William the Conqueror caused a stir by bequeathing England to his second surviving son. On hearing his father's wishes, William rushed to England and secured the throne before any opposition could be organized. He was crowned on 26 September by Archbishop Lanfranc, and had little trouble suppressing the baronial uprising in favour of his elder brother, Robert, Duke of Normandy. The division of England and Normandy caused problems for both brothers. Many of their chief subjects held land on both sides of the English Channel, and therefore owed allegiance to two over-lords. Having secured England, William tried to turn the tables and deprive Robert of Normandy. There followed about five years of confused manoeuverings with William fighting Robert and their younger brother Henry, or Robert and William fighting Henry, or Henry and William fighting Robert. King Philip of France invariably supported whoever was fighting William.

William had been his father's favourite son. He was short, stocky and

Manuscript   British Museum

William II

red haired, with such a ruddy complexion he was nicknamed Rufus. He was barely literate and in public he stammered so badly that when he was excited or angry he was almost inarticulate. There was a strong streak of cruelty and coarseness in his nature. He never married and some say that he was a homosexual.

In 1089 Archbishop Lanfranc died. The Tudor historian Holinshed wrote of him that he was 'a wise, politic and learned prelate, who, whilst he lived, mollified the furious and cruel nature of King William Rufus.' The dominant figure at court now became Ranulf Flambard, William's chaplain. Flambard was a humbly-born Norman who had become a priest as the quickest way to social and political advancement. He had ingratiated himself with the King by pointing out ingenious devices for swelling the royal exchequer, and was rewarded with the post of Justiciar and later with the bishopric of Durham. Flambard encouraged the King to make no appointments to vacant bishoprics and abbacies and to divert their revenues into the royal coffers. After Lanfranc's death William enjoyed a handsome profit from the rich See of Canterbury, treating the petitions of the clergy for a new Primate with scorn and derision.

In 1093 a serious illness frightened the King into patching up his quarrel with the Church. The gentle, saintly Anselm, Bishop of Bec, was dragged to his bedside, had the ring forced upon his finger and the crozier thrust into his hand, while the bishops sang a Te Deum in the royal bedchamber. 'You would yoke me,' complained Anselm, 'a poor feeble old sheep, with the savage bull.' Anselm had good cause to be reluctant, for as the King's health improved his fear of God diminished, and according to Holinshed he again became 'very cruel and inconstant in all his doings, so that he became a heavy burden unto his people.' Bitter quarrels broke out. Anselm fiercely denounced the vices of the court and Flambard's extortionate methods, and an acrimonious dispute developed over the military service owed by the See of Canterbury to the crown. Anselm stuck to his principles, but lacked Lanfranc's diplomatic tact in maintaining the uneasy concordat between the Church and the crown. After four years he gave up the struggle and went off to Rome. The delighted King seized Anselm's estates, saying, 'tell the Archbishop that I hated him yesterday, I hate him the more today and shall hate him even more tomorrow.'

Although William Rufus is invariably portrayed as a bad King, he maintained firm control of his kingdom and strengthened the power of the monarchy during his reign. For four years he also ruled Normandy, for in

1096 his brother Robert pawned the Duchy to him so that he could afford to take part in the first Crusade.

On 2 August 1100 the King went hunting red deer in the New Forest with a group of companions, including his younger brother Henry. Later that day a charcoal burner found the King lying with an arrow in his heart. A few peasants carried the body to Winchester in a cart, where it was unceremoniously and hastily buried. According to the chronicler, William of Malmesbury, the King and one of his knights, Walter Tyrrell, became separated from the rest of the party and were chasing a hart when 'Walter let fly an arrow which shaved the hair on the animal's back, sped on and wounded the King standing beyond.' Others say that Tyrrell's arrow glanced off a tree and struck the King. Whatever the truth of the matter, Tyrrell fled to France denying that he had anything to do with the King's death, while Prince Henry made straight for Winchester to gain possession of the royal treasury, and from there to London and the throne.

Henry I 1100–1135

It is said that as his father lay dying, Henry carefully checked the weight of the £5,000 worth of silver coin bequeathed to him. He is an interesting example of how a shrewd, cruel and unattractive man can become a successful and popular king. In spite of his oath of allegiance to his elder brother Robert, Henry set out, with sound political instinct, to win the support of the people. He made lavish gifts to the barons from the treasury, imprisoned Flambard in the Tower of London and recalled Anselm to take up his post again as Archbishop of Canterbury. He also issued a charter of liberties promising to redress grievances, to rule justly and to abide by the old customs of the country. As the crowning act of ingratiation with his English subjects, Henry married Edith, the penniless but well-connected daughter of Malcolm III of Scotland. Through her mother Margaret, Edith was a direct descendant of Alfred the Great, and owing to this marriage all the subsequent English sovereigns except Stephen are descended from the ancient royal House of Wessex. As Edith's name was difficult for Normans to pronounce, Henry changed it to Matilda.

In 1101 Robert, Duke of Normandy, returned from the Crusades and landed at Portsmouth to claim the crown. He was joined by several powerful barons, and the irrepressible Flambard who had escaped from prison, but through the mediation of Anselm, the brothers were temporarily reconciled. Robert agreed to accept a substantial pension in return for recognizing Henry as King of England, and Henry agreed to forgive his rebellious subjects. But Henry was not inclined either to pay the pension or forgive the rebels. He ruthlessly suppressed those who had supported Robert until 'no man in England dared . . . hold any castle against him.' In 1106 he crossed to France and, to the delight of his English subjects, inflicted a devastating defeat on the Normans at Tinchebrai. Henry now assumed control of Normandy and imprisoned his brother Robert in Cardiff Castle. Robert died in 1134 having spent almost thirty years in prison, and was buried in Gloucester Cathedral.

Henry was a good administrator, keen on efficiency and order. He appointed gifted and able men to the service of the crown, regardless of their social origins. Such a man was Roger, Bishop of Salisbury, who organized a department at court for the collection of royal revenue. A chequered cloth was used to facilitate counting, the department became known as the Exchequer, and the position of Chancellor of the Exchequer was soon one of the most powerful in the King's Household. Exchequer officials would travel around the country settling local financial disputes as well as ensuring the proper administration of the King's justice. Henry strengthened the traditional local assemblies – the Shire and Hundred courts – to the detriment of the feudal courts controlled by the local lords, and although his motivation was self-interest, Henry won the title 'Lion of Justice'. Better educated than most men of his day, he was also known as Beauclerc, or 'fine scholar'.

Although Henry did much to stabilize the monarchy in England, he was particularly unfortunate in that, although he had fathered at least twenty-one children, only his son William and daughter Matilda were legitimate. In 1120, Prince William was returning to England from a visit to Normandy in the newly-built *White Ship* when it was wrecked off the Norman coast. Evidently the captain and most of his crew were drunk and all on board were drowned except a butcher from Rouen. Henry married again, but the second marriage was childless. In an attempt to secure the peaceful descent of the crown, he made his barons swear that when he died they would accept his daughter Matilda as their Queen. In 1127 he pushed his daughter into a match with Geoffrey of Blois, Count of Anjou, his

Manuscript   *British Museum*

Henry I

BALSAM LAKE PUBLIC LIBRARY

neighbour on the southern border of Normandy. The wedding was unpopular with the Anglo-Norman nobles but two years later Matilda produced a son, and again Henry induced the barons to acknowledge her as heir to the throne.

In 1135 the King was again in Normandy, hunting at Lyons-la-Foret, when he got indigestion after eating 'a surfeit of lampreys'. He developed a fever and died within three days. His body was brought back to England and he was buried in the monastery he had founded at Reading.

Matilda

Matilda had been betrothed and after much delay married to the Holy Roman Emperor Henry V. It was a childless marriage and after eleven years of wedlock, Matilda was left a widow, although still only twenty-five. She then returned to England in 1125 to be recognized as heir to the throne at a meeting of the *Curia Regis*, or Great Council. Her father negotiated a second marriage with fifteen-year-old Geoffrey, Count of Anjou, called Geoffrey Plantagenet because he wore a sprig of broom or 'planta genista' in his helmet as his cognizance. The King received the news that the royal pair had a child with delight, for he foresaw the time when his grandson, Henry, would unite England, Normandy and Anjou. But when the news of King Henry's death reached England in 1135, the Great Council chose Stephen as King. Matilda and her husband were rejected as 'aliens'.

Matilda was not the woman to be rejected by anyone. Described as a fierce, proud, hard and cynical woman with a passionate interest in politics, one contemporary wrote that 'she had the nature of a man in the frame of a woman.' Matilda and Geoffrey were in Anjou when Henry died, and when Stephen was crowned they appealed to the Pope in Rome without success. They spent the next few years trying to enforce Matilda's claim to Normandy. In England, Stephen was proving incapable of controlling the barons, particularly Henry's illegitimate son, Robert, Earl of Gloucester. He lost the support of the bishops, and anarchy reigned. Matilda lost no time in taking advantage of the situation and landed in

England on 22 September 1139, accompanied by her half-brother, Robert of Gloucester. Civil war broke out. Some fought for Stephen, some for Matilda and some for themselves. The *Anglo-Saxon Chronicle* grimly described the situation: 'The barons filled their castles with devils and evil men. They took those men whom they thought had any property, both by night and day, even peasant men and women, and put them in prison for their gold and silver, and tortured them with unutterable tortures. Never yet had there been more wretchedness in the land, nor did heathen men ever do worse than they did. Men said openly that Christ and his saints slept.'

After two years of fighting, Stephen was defeated and captured at Lincoln, and Matilda was proclaimed 'Lady and Queen of England', but she was never crowned. Before the coronation could take place she quarrelled with the Church and alienated many of her supporters, who claimed that she 'behaved like an empress when she was not quite a queen.' The people of London drove her from the capital, and welcomed the other Matilda, Stephen's wife, in her stead. Soon her supporters were routed by those of Stephen at Winchester. Stephen was thereupon released and Matilda's cause steadily declined. She returned to Normandy in 1147, retiring from the scene of struggle and leaving her young son Henry to continue on her behalf.

Matilda mellowed as she grew older, turning from politics to religion, although she acted as a very able regent for her son Henry II during the first few years of his reign. Matilda died on 30 January 1167, and was buried at Bec in Normandy. On her tombstone are inscribed the words she composed herself: Here lies Henry's daughter, wife and mother; great by birth, greater by marriage, greatest by motherhood.

Stephen 1135–1154

None of William the Conqueror's sons was survived by a male heir, but his daughter Adela, who married the Count of Blois, had a son, Stephen. Henry I had much favoured his nephew and had arranged a marriage between him and Matilda, the heiress to the rich county of Boulogne. Stephen also had lands in England and Normandy, and with the other members of the Great Council he had promised to recognize his cousin, Henry's daughter Matilda, as the lawful heir to the throne. But when Henry died, Matilda was in Anjou and Stephen made a bold bid for the crown. He had several things in his favour. There was widespread reluctance to have a female ruler; many disliked Matilda's Angevin connection; many of the late King's advisers, including most of the clergy, were prepared to back Stephen. Stephen sped to England from Blois and, as the chronicler Henry of Huntingdon put it, was crowned 'in the twinkling of an eye', by the Archbishop of Canterbury at Westminster Abbey. From there the King moved to Oxford where he held Court. To secure his position Stephen made rash promises to all the estates of the realm. He allowed the barons the right to fortify their castles, and to the common man he promised relief of taxation and a restoration of the laws of Edward the Confessor. Stephen thus curtailed his own royal powers at a time when he needed them most. When Stephen thought he was buying friends he was actually buying time.

William of Malmesbury described the new King as 'an energetic man but lacking in judgement, an active soldier at his best in a difficult situation, lenient to his enemies and courteous to all. Good at making promises, but not so good at keeping them.' Stephen soon had trouble on his hands. The *Anglo-Saxon Chronicle*, referring to the barons, states: 'When the traitors perceived a mild man and soft and good and did no justice then did they all manner of horrors.' Stephen was his own worst enemy. He was quite unable to control the feuding barons, and when Matilda landed in England to contest his claim to the throne, civil war

Stephen

broke out. Tall, with a good physique, Stephen was a courageous, even reckless, soldier, but although he won victories, he often failed to follow them through. A contemporary, Walter Map, said the King was 'of outstanding skill in arms, but in other things almost an idiot.'

The chroniclers described in grim detail the 'nineteen long winters' of Stephen's reign, when 'the north was harried and pillaged by the Scots, the rich cornlands of the south were spoiled by foreign mercenaries which both sides employed and the whole country was given over to rapine, torture and arson.' Even after his cousin Matilda left England in 1148, the civil war continued in a desultory fashion. Matilda's sixteen-year-old son Henry made a further attempt to oust Stephen in 1149, but he was unsuccessful and returned to Normandy. Stephen sought recognition for his son Eustace as lawful heir to the throne, but the bishops refused to accept him. In 1153 Henry Plantagenet returned to England with an army. Henry was now almost as powerful as the King of France, having acquired Normandy, Anjou and Maine from his parents and Aquitaine and Poitou from his wife. Henry swept all before him and was greeted as a saviour. When Eustace died that same year, Stephen capitulated. A compromise was achieved at Wallingford by which it was agreed that Stephen should reign until his death and that Henry should help him restore peace and good government, and succeed him to the throne at his death. Stephen had less than a year in which to enjoy the fruits of peace. Nine months later, on 24 October 1154, he died at Dover. He was buried in the Abbey he had founded at Faversham, but his tomb was destroyed during Henry VIII's dissolution of the monasteries 'for the trifling gain of the lead'.

Henry II 1154–1189

Henry was born to power. His mother Matilda was heir to the throne of England and the Duchy of Normandy. His father Geoffrey was Count of Anjou and Maine. By 1151 he had inherited everything except England. In 1152 he married Eleanor of Aquitaine within weeks of her divorce from Louis VII of France. The union made Henry Duke of Aquitaine and Count of Poitou, and two years later he succeeded Stephen to the throne of England.

Henry was crowned on 19 December at Westminster Abbey. He was twenty-one years old, short and thick-set, with bandy legs attributed to endless riding. He took little interest in his personal appearance, and his cloak, like his hair, was cut unfashionably short, earning him the name 'curtmantle'. He was well educated and had an alert and restless mind. The chronicler Walter Map said that Henry understood every language spoken between the English Channel and the River Jordan, and that his Latin was as fluent as his French. Henry's mental and physical energy seems to have been boundless. He was never still, even transacting business in church during the sermon. He was stimulating and exciting but also infuriating. Peter of Blois, one of his courtiers, wrote: 'If the King had announced that he was going to stay all day, he was certain to leave early in the morning. If on the other hand he ordered an early start, he was equally certain to remain where he was till mid-day. I hardly dare say so, but I think he did it on purpose.'

Henry's first task in England was to re-establish the King's authority and justice. He involved his barons in legislation and policy-making, re-established the tours of the assize judges and laid the foundations of English Common Law.

He travelled constantly. Henry's old enemy, Louis VII of France, complained that he was 'now in Ireland, now in England, now in Normandy; he must fly rather than travel by horse or ship.' Yet Henry's effective government did not suffer through his restlessness. He appointed

Henry II

32

brilliant men to the service of the crown, and made but one fatal error of judgement. When the old Archbishop of Canterbury died in 1162, he nominated his Chancellor and old friend, Thomas Becket, for the position. Thomas was not a man to do things by halves. He warned Henry that he would work as hard for the Church as he had for the King. Henry would not believe him and found himself for the next eight years involved in bitter disputes with Thomas, culminating in his violent outburst against 'that turbulent priest', which set in train the terrible murder of the Archbishop in Canterbury Cathedral by four of Henry's knights. Henry found Thomas stronger in death than in life. Within three years Thomas had been canonized and Henry submitted to a humiliating public scourging at his tomb.

Henry's quarrel with Becket overshadowed many of the achievements of his reign. In 1173 he put down a rebellion inspired by his son Henry and began a programme of castle-building that was to ensure the maintenance of law and order in his kingdom. He abandoned the motte-and-bailey of earth and timber in favour of the rectangular stone towers that dominated the surrounding countryside. Henry allowed those knights who did not want to fulfil their military obligations to give money instead, with which he could hire mercenaries. He also established his over-lordship of Ireland and through the marriages of his three daughters set up links with the King of Sicily, the King of Castile and the Prince of Saxony.

Yet Henry could not control his own family. His wife Eleanor had come to hate him because of his undisguised infidelities, and she did her utmost to turn her sons against their father. Henry once caught sight of a fresco at Winchester showing four young eagles attacking an old one, and observed: 'Those eaglets are my sons who are harrying me to death.' In different combinations, the sons rebelled against their father four times, actively encouraged by the King of France. Richard, his mother's favourite, defeated Henry at Le Mans and forced him to submit to a humiliating treaty. When Henry was told that his youngest son John, upon whom he had lavished excessive affection, had also joined forces against him, he gave up. Sick with blood-poisoning from a wound in his heel, Henry retired to Chinon, in his old homeland of Anjou, where he died on 6 July 1189, murmuring, 'Shame, shame on a conquered King.' He was buried at his favourite Abbey of Fontevrault.

Richard I 1189–1199

When Richard, Henry's eldest surviving son, received the news of his father's death he went to Fontevrault to see the body. It is recorded that while he was in the church, blood flowed from the nostrils of the dead King. It was generally believed at the time that a murdered man bleeds in the presence of his murderer. Henry had cursed Richard before he died and many believed that Richard's actions had hastened Henry's death. The old King had made no provision for the succession, and it passed naturally to Richard without being contested. Richard's coronation took place on 3 September 1189. It was a magnificent occasion. The King strode down the aisle of Westminster Abbey under a silk canopy held by four of his barons. He was a tall striking figure with fair hair and blue eyes, and reputed to be one of the greatest soldiers in Christendom.

But Richard's sights were set beyond Christian Europe. In 1187 the Mahommedan leader Saladin had captured Jerusalem and the Pope called on all Christian rulers to take up arms on behalf of their brothers in Jerusalem and retrieve the Holy Land from the Saracens. The Crusades appealed to all the instincts of a man like Richard: military adventures in distant lands, under the guise of being a sacred enterprise blessed by the Church. After his coronation, Richard applied himself to raising enough money to take part in the Third Crusade. He sold honours, privileges and positions in Church and state. He sold charters to the more important English towns, thus encouraging the growth of municipal self-government – of which one important result was the appearance of the first Mayor of London. He is quoted as saying, 'I would sell London itself if I could find a purchaser rich enough.' He sailed from England on 12 December leaving his mother Eleanor and William Longchamps to run the country. 'Almost everyone,' says the chronicler, 'was angered that a noble king about to set out to distant regions should leave his own kingdom with so little ceremony and should have, as he left it, so much less care for it than he ought.' Richard had only got as far as Sicily when trouble broke out, so he sent back his father's old servant, Walter of Coutances, to govern the country for him. It took Richard two years to get to the Holy Land. A large part of this time was spent in Sicily where he went as a guest of its ruler Tancred. After a dispute with his fellow-crusader Philip of France, he captured the island. He also seized Cyprus when two of his ships were wrecked off the coast and the crews ill-treated by the islanders. While in Cyprus he married Berengaria of Navarre.

On 12 July 1191 the Crusaders relieved the siege of Acre. The victory was marred by dissension in the Christian ranks. Duke Leopold of Austria had placed his standard next to those of Richard and King Philip Augustus of France on the walls of the conquered city, and was deeply offended when Richard removed it. Philip and Richard quarrelled over who would be made King of Jerusalem when it was captured. When Philip went home, taking Duke Leopold with him, Richard carried on as sole commander of the crusading forces. His skill and courage struck terror into the hearts of the Saracens and won the admiration of Saladin. In spite of some remarkable military successes, Richard failed to take Jerusalem. According to tradition, he stood on the hill of Emmaus overlooking the city but held his shield before his eyes so that he could not see it, declaring, 'O Lord God, suffer not my eyes to behold thy Holy City, since I cannot deliver it from the hands of thy enemies.' Richard met Saladin on Mount Tabor to conclude a truce to last three years, three months, three days and three hours. During that time, Christian pilgrims were to be allowed free access to Jerusalem.

Richard left Acre in October 1192 having acquired a reputation for bravery and chivalry, and the romantic title 'Lion Heart'. He was ship-wrecked in the Adriatic and had to make his way through Germany in disguise because he feared capture at the hands of Duke Leopold. He was seized by the Duke's soldiers at an inn near Vienna. The Duke's over-lord, the Holy Roman Emperor Henry VI, demanded the famous captive, saying, 'a duke has no right to imprison a king; that is the privilege only of an emperor.' Henry held Richard captive until the first instalment of the huge ransom of 150,000 marks had been paid. Philip Augustus of France and Richard's brother John intrigued to delay the King's release, but England and Normandy were taxed to raise the money, and after a year in prison Richard was set free. When he heard the news, Philip Augustus sent John a message: 'Have a care – the Devil is unloosed.'

Richard returned to England on 13 March 1194. It says a great deal for the administrative achievements of Henry II that the country had not fallen

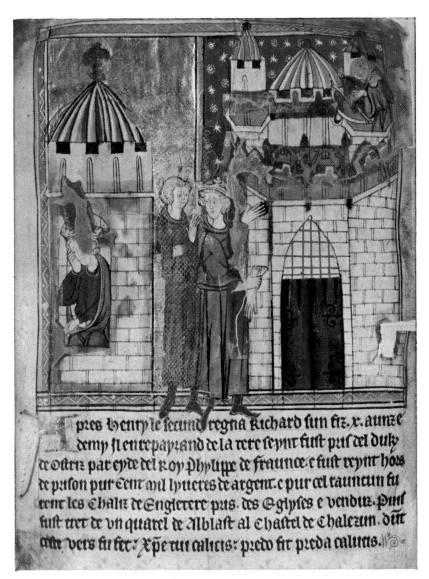

Richard I

Manuscript

John

37

into anarchic chaos during the absence of its ruler. In spite of John's attempts to seize the throne, Richard was well served by his advisers and John fled to France. Richard forgave his brother, and after staying long enough in England to raise yet more money from his long-suffering subjects, he spent the last years of his reign fighting the King of France. He left Hubert Walter, Archbishop of Canterbury, who had been trained by Henry II's lawyers, to govern England for him. Hubert was a brilliant administrator and carried on Henry II's legal and financial reforms, in particular further developing the jury system and the local responsibilities of the knights of the shires.

On the continent of Europe Richard continued to win acclaim for his fighting feats, although as his companion de Born commented, he was hunting an eagle with a sparrow hawk. During a petty quarrel with a vassal, the Viscount of Limoges, he was struck in the shoulder by a crossbow bolt and died a few days later. Richard and Berengaria had no children, and so the dying King had named John as his heir. He also asked for his heart to be buried at Rouen and his body to be laid at his father's feet at Fontevrault. Berengaria devoted herself to good works and eventually retired to a convent. Richard the Lion Heart had been King of England for ten years but had spent less than one year in his kingdom.

John 1199–1216

Arthur of Brittany was heir to the throne of England. His father Geoffrey had died in 1186 and his uncle, King Richard, had wanted to educate him at the English court. But his mother Constance did not trust her brother-in-law and brought Arthur up in Brittany. Richard on his deathbed declared that his youngest brother John should succeed him, and this John had little trouble in doing. Twelve-year-old Arthur was in Brittany when Richard died and only Anjou declared for him. John was thirty-two years old and able to secure the support of the Archbishop of Canterbury in England and the possession of Richard's treasure at Chinon. He had himself crowned as Duke of Normandy at Rouen and as King of England at Westminster Abbey.

Contemporary historians have loudly condemned John as a bad King and a bad man, but it must be remembered that most of the contemporary historians were monastic chroniclers and severe on a King who showed his contempt for the Church. 'He did evil in the sight of the Lord,' declared one chronicler, 'on such a scale that Hell was made fouler when John died.' Another wrote that in a rage 'his eyes darted fire and his countenance became livid.' Many mention his greed, violence, treachery, malice, sloth and immorality. And yet other records show that John was a brilliant, highly cultivated man who loved his books, showed himself to be a competent soldier at times and protective towards such thirteenth-century underdogs as scholars, Jews and animals. Above all, John was exceedingly unlucky. He had against him the two strongest men in Europe: Pope Innocent III, who had spiritual as well as temporal powers at his disposal, and Philip Augustus, King of France.

Soon after his accession, John deeply offended the English nobility by divorcing Avice of Gloucester, the richest heiress in England, whom he had married in 1189. By abducting and marrying Isabella, daughter of the Count of Angoulême, who was betrothed to Hugh of Lusignan, he alienated French nobility, and the French King declared John's French lands forfeit. Stung into unaccustomed energy, John crossed to France, and in one coup captured several Poitevin knights, his rival, Hugh of Lusignan, and his own nephew Arthur. John dispatched the knights to Corfe Castle, where they starved to death, Hugh was imprisoned in Bristol Castle, and Arthur was asked to renounce his claim to the English throne. He told John, 'I will never give you a year's peace till I have won back England and all my uncle Richard's inheritance.' Arthur was seventeen years old. John imprisoned him in Rouen where he was murdered, presumably at John's order, a few months later. Philip Augustus of France then invaded Normandy, which John made little effort to save, and John's subjects sorely felt this humiliation. All that was left of Henry II's vast French empire was Gascony and the Channel Islands.

John next proceeded to quarrel with the Pope. In a row over the appointment of the new Archbishop of Canterbury England was placed under an interdict and John was excommunicated. When the Pope called on Philip of France to drive John from the throne, John gave in. In May 1213 John resigned his crown to the Papal Legate, Pandulf, who kept it for four days and then gave it back to John as a sign that he held his kingdom as a papal fief.

After this further loss of face at home, John made an abortive attempt to regain Normandy. He destroyed the French fleet but retreated in disarray after the battle of Bouvines in 1214. The English barons were becoming increasingly agitated with the King's arbitrary behaviour, and they found a leader in Archbishop Stephen Langton, who reminded them of their rights as embodied in Henry I's coronation charter. John was forced to put his seal to the 'Articles of the Barons' – the *Magna Carta* – at Runnymede on 15 June 1215, declaring that his subjects wanted to set up 'twenty-five kings in England'. The Pope released John from this oath taken under duress, and the King then set out to punish the rebels. With his mercenary troops, he conducted a campaign of vengeance against his barons. In October he set out from East Anglia to cross the Wash where the estuary is dry at low tide. The tide came up unexpectedly and all the King's wagons and mules carrying his stores and treasures were lost. If the beautiful thirteenth-century gold and silver cup (see title page) dredged up in the Wash and kept at King's Lynn belonged to John, then his treasure was very fine indeed. Overwhelmed with anger at his loss, John is said to have gorged himself that night on fruit and cider. He died of dysentery a week later on 18 October, and was buried in Worcester Cathedral. Four years after his death his widow, Isabella, finally married Hugh of Lusignan.

Henry III 1216–1272

Henry III at nine was the youngest King so far to wear the crown of England, albeit a makeshift one, as the real one lay at the bottom of the Wash with the rest of King John's treasure. As London was in the hands of the French Dauphin Louis, Henry had to be crowned in Gloucester Cathedral. The *Magna Carta* was re-issued and the young King called on his barons to forget the troubles of the past. The barons would have looked foolish had they carried on fighting for a Frenchman in England when their old adversary was dead and they had no quarrel with his son. Louis had been elated at John's death, expecting to take the kingdom without much difficulty, and was taken aback to find his English supporters deserting him. After the Battle of Lincoln in 1217, Louis went home and

Manuscript

Henry III

British Museum

Henry's regent, William the Marshal, Earl of Pembroke, expelled the foreign mercenaries and restored peace.

When William the Marshal died in 1219, Hubert de Burgh, another of the experienced older barons, took over the government while the young King was educated by Peter des Roches, Bishop of Winchester. Hubert de Burgh ruled wisely and successfully, and although Henry was declared to be of age in 1227 he did not actually assert his personal rule until 1232, when he dismissed de Burgh, whom he blamed for the failure of an abortive expedition to France in 1230.

With the fall of Hubert de Burgh, Henry was accused of putting England once more into the hands of foreigners. Henry found himself drawn to the cultivated and sophisticated French and Italians who came to his court firstly through Peter des Roches and secondly through his wife, Eleanor of Provence, whom he married in 1236. She brought to her husband a love of troubadour poetry and a host of greedy relatives to whom Henry handed out important Church and state positions. The chronicler Matthew Paris wrote with great hostility about the foreign influence at Henry's court and the grievances felt by the English nobility. The situation was aggravated by the high-handed treatment of the English Church by the Pope. Italians were appointed to vacancies traditionally held by Englishmen, and matters came to a head when the Pope offered Henry the crown of Sicily for his second son Edmund in exchange for a large sum of money. The King could not resist the offer but was unable to raise the money himself, and the barons were determined to exact wide concessions in return for granting it. The barons found a leader in Simon de Montfort, Earl of Leicester, although he was a Frenchman and the King's brother-in-law. In 1258 they forced the Provisions of Oxford on the King, which virtually put the country into the hands of a feudal oligarchy. When Henry went back on the agreement, de Montfort organized open rebellion, and at the battle of Lewes in 1264 found himself master of England. In 1265 he summoned a 'Parliament' to which he called the barons he could trust, the prelates of the realm, two knights from each shire and two noted citizens from certain boroughs. This historic meeting was a milestone in the foundation of democracy.

The King's supporters now began to re-form under the leadership of Henry's eldest son Edward who defeated and killed de Montfort at the battle of Evesham in August 1265. A compromise was reached between Edward and the barons and for the last few years of Henry's long reign, Edward ruled in all but name.

Henry and his Queen had always been devoted to each other and with their two sons and three daughters led an unusually happy family life, and Edward had great love and respect for his father. Matthew Paris, one of the most important medieval historians, roundly condemned Henry's weakness and lack of statesmanship. He wrote that the King had a heart of wax, although he was not cruel or malicious like his father. In the *Divina Comedia* Dante puts Henry in the limbo of ineffectual souls, a region in Purgatory reserved for simpletons and children. Henry loved beauty above everything else and surrounded himself with artists and craftsmen who were engaged on the new gothic rebuilding at Westminster Abbey and the chapel at Windsor Castle, as well as many other church buildings throughout the country. Henry revered Edward the Confessor, for whom he had a magnificent new shrine built behind the high altar of Westminster Abbey, and himself acted as pall-bearer when Edward's coffin was moved. Nicholas Trivet has left a description of Henry in his *Annales Sex Regum Anglie*: 'He was . . . of moderate stature, of compact body, with the lid of one eye rather drooping, so that it concealed part of the blackness of the pupil; robust in strength, but impulsive in action.' Henry died on 16 November 1272 and was buried in the grave formerly occupied by Edward the Confessor in Westminster Abbey.

Manuscript   British Museum

Edward I

44

Edward I 1272–1307

As the body of Henry III was being lowered into the grave, the barons in turn placed their hands on it and swore allegiance to the King's eldest son Edward, who was absent on a crusade. Edward had been away for two years before his father died, and was to spend another two years coming home. Yet his accession was accepted without question and he was proclaimed King four days after Henry's death on the basis of his hereditary right and the acceptance of the barons. On their arrival in England in August 1274 Edward and his wife, Eleanor of Castile, were received 'with all joy that might be devised. The streets were hung with rich cloths of silk, arras and tapestry; the aldermen and burgesses of the city threw out of their window handfuls of gold and silver to signify the great gladness which they conceived of his safe return.' Edward clearly was a man of stature and authority. Nicholas Trivet wrote that he 'was a man of tried prudence in the transaction of affairs, devoted from his earliest years to the practice of arms. Hence he had won that fame as a knight in diverse lands which gave him a transcendent place among Christian princes.

'He was handsome, and so tall that he stood head and shoulders above most people. His hair, light and silvery when he was a boy, turned very dark in manhood, and as he grew old, became as white as a swan. He had a broad brow and symmetrical features except that a droop of the left eyelid recalled his father's appearance. He was persuasive and ready in speech, in spite of his lisp. His long arms with their powerful and agile play enabled him to become a swordsman second to none; his chest projected beyond his belly, and his longshanks gave him his firm seat in the saddle, and his mastery over the most spirited thoroughbred.'

Although Edward's wife came as a foreign princess to England, she possessed great charm and tact and won the love of the common people and the deep affection of her husband. When later in Edward's reign she died suddenly in Lincoln, the King's grief was so great that he raised a magnificent cross at every place where her coffin rested on its way to London.

Edward had always cherished the ambition to assert English sovereignty over Wales and Scotland, and the years 1275–94 were occupied with carefully organized campaigns against the Welsh. The subjugation of the country was marked by the erection of the huge castles of Caernarvon and Conway and many others such as Harlech, Beaumaris and Caerphilly. Builders came from every corner of Britain, often with their wives and children, to work on them, and the so-called 'Edwardian' castles marked the high-watermark of fortified architecture and impregnability. The annexation of Wales was marked by the Statute of 1284, and that same year Queen Eleanor gave birth in Caernarvon Castle to a son and heir with whom began the custom of conferring the title of Prince of Wales upon the sovereign's eldest son.

In 1286 Edward seized the opportunity afforded by the disputed claim to the Scottish throne on the death of Alexander III to mount an attack on Scotland. He led an army north three times, and though he was successful in battle, the Scots remained unconquered. As one chronicler wrote: 'every winter undid every summer's work.' During this period relations with France deteriorated and came to a head when Philip the Fair tricked Edward into giving up Gascony. The Welsh picked this moment to rebel, and the need to obtain money for his wars led Edward in 1295 to summon the largest and most representative of any parliament yet, which became known as the Model Parliament.

In 1306 Scotland found a new champion in Robert Bruce, and Edward, though seriously ill, went north, carried on a litter, to deal with him. News of Bruce's successes so infuriated the old King that near the border he insisted on riding at the head of his army into Scotland, but never arrived. At the border town of Burgh-on-Sands he collapsed through sheer exhaustion, but before he died on 7 July he ordered his son to boil the body, extract the bones and carry them with the army until the Scots had been subdued. Edward's son disobeyed his father's command and buried him in Westminster Abbey under a plain slab on which was inscribed: *Edwardus Primus Scottorum malleus hic est*: Here lies Edward I the Hammer of the Scots.

Edward II 1307–1327

The medieval barons liked a strong king who could win wars. In Edward II they got a weak king, graceful but effeminate, and quite incapable of dealing with his inheritance of war, debt, easily aggrieved barons and hostile Scots. He made a half-hearted attempt to pursue the Scottish war but gave up when he reached Ayrshire, and went home. At twenty-three he was already something of an eccentric and it was even rumoured that Edward was not really the King's son but a changeling, the son of an obscure carter. But in appearance Edward was very like his father, being tall, good-looking and physically very strong. He had bright curly hair and a quick tongue, but was naïve, extravagant and devoted to a childhood friend, Piers Gaveston from Gascony, whom Edward I had banished from the court. Edward's first act as King was to recall Gaveston and make him Earl of Cornwall. Gaveston was fascinating, witty and vain. He lived like a prince and took great delight in mocking the English nobles at court, and added fuel to the fire of their hatred by invariably trouncing them in tournaments.

When Edward went to France for his marriage to Princess Isabella – she was sixteen years old and reputedly one of the most beautiful women of her day, although also known as the she-wolf of France – the King appointed Gaveston as Regent in his absence, which united the barons in their common hatred of the King's favourite, and further alienated them from the King. The barons twice forced Edward to banish Gaveston, but each time he returned. In 1312 Gaveston was captured at Scarborough, tried illegally at Warwick Castle, and to Edward's great grief, murdered by the 'black dog of Arden', the Earl of Warwick, on 1 July 1312.

In Scotland Robert Bruce had been steadily gaining ground, and by 1314 the only castle left in English hands was Stirling, and that was under siege. In response to a desperate appeal from the Governor, Edward gathered an army and marched north, but had little baronial support. It transpired later that Thomas of Lancaster had been in treasonable

Tomb effigy   *Gloucester Cathedral*

Edward II

48

correspondence with Robert Bruce and deliberately stayed away from the campaign. The whole thing was badly mismanaged and the English army was slaughtered on the marshy ground of Bannockburn. Edward himself narrowly escaped and Robert Bruce said of his victory, 'I am more afraid of the father dead than of the son alive. By all the saints, it was more difficult to get half a foot of land from the old King than a whole kingdom from the son.'

Bannockburn was followed by years of terrible harvests and famine. The baronial faction under Thomas of Lancaster was all-powerful, and Edward turned for support to a new favourite, Hugh Despencer, and his father. He took advantage of baronial bickering to try to control the government, and civil war broke out. Edward defeated the Lancastrian faction at Boroughbridge in 1322, and executed Thomas of Lancaster in his own castle at Pontefract.

But Edward had not learned from experience, and again alienated his supporters through his over-indulgence of the Despencers. His wife Isabella, who had openly supported Lancaster in the past, now began to plot against the King with her lover, Roger Mortimer. On the pretext of seeing her brother, the King of France, she left England to join the exiled Mortimer, and became the new focus for discontent. Mortimer and the Queen returned to England in 1326 with an army of mercenaries and the custody of the young Prince Edward. This time, Edward was bullied into abdicating by the use of threats against his children. Edward did not lack courage and to the embarrassment of his tormentors he was, at forty-three, strong enough to survive systematic deprivation and torture. He was moved from castle to castle, and on 22 September 1327 was murdered in Berkeley in Gloucestershire. Red hot irons were passed through his body and his bowels burnt out, although there appeared no outward cause of death. The following day the castle gates were thrown open and people were invited to see the body of the late King. But the King's terrible screams had rent the Gloucestershire countryside, and many, according to Holinshed 'prayed heartily to God to receive his soul, for they understood by those cries what the matter meant.'

With Edward's pitiful death ends one of the most dismal and distasteful chapters of English history.

Edward III 1327–1377

Edward III was fourteen when he ascended the throne, and it was four years before he felt confident enough to overthrow Mortimer and control his mother's excesses. The pair's outrageous extravagance and misuse of power made them far more unpopular than Edward II had ever been. In October 1330, ignoring his mother's plea to 'spare the gentle Mortimer', Edward had the treacherous man arrested and tried for turning Isabella against her husband, for murdering Edward II and for seizing the government. He was hanged on 29 November and Isabella was dispatched to confinement in Castle Rising in Norfolk. After his father's ignominious end and his mother's sordid regency, Edward seemed heaven-sent, and England took a turn for the better. Edward's Queen, to whom he was devoted, was immensely popular and soon presented him with a son, Edward of Woodstock, while the King himself, vigorous and attractive, was the embodiment of medieval chivalry. In fulfilment of a vow to restore King Arthur's Round Table, Edward instituted the Order of the Garter in 1348, with its commanding motto: *Honi soit qui mal y pense* (Evil be to him who evil thinks), which the King is reputed to have said when stooping to pick up a lady's garter.

The French chronicler Froissart describes Edward's colourful and brilliant court with its elaborate tournaments – the outward expression of this age of chivalry – where fully armed and mounted knights would engage in war-like games for fun, prestige and a favour from the ladies who looked on. But Edward was anxious to prove himself on a real battlefield. In the 1330s he fought hard to impose a puppet king on the Scots but eventually gave up and turned to the more exciting prospect of conquering France. In 1328 Charles II, Edward's maternal uncle, died leaving no male heir. Charles's cousin Philip IV succeeded to the French throne, but Edward contested the succession, writing to Philip that '. . . we propose to recover the right we have to that inheritance, which you violently withhold from us', and challenged him to single combat. Philip ignored the challenge and deliberately provoked Edward into a war. Philip befriended the Scots, attacked Gascony and tried to block the vital wool trade. In 1337 he declared the English lands in France forfeited and French ships attacked the English coast; and so began that disastrous period of hostilities that was to be known as the Hundred Years War. To begin with things went well for England. At Sluys, Crécy and Poitiers Edward won outstanding victories, the English longbow proving superior to French armour. In 1360 a truce was signed at Brétigny whereby Edward renounced his claim to France in return for Guienne, Calais and a huge ransom for the French King whom he had captured at Poitiers.

The war had taxed English resources to the limit, and Edward was always desperately short of money. Apart from borrowing huge sums from the Lombard banking houses, he called forty-eight parliaments. It became common practice for the lower house, meeting separately for the first time, to demand redress of grievances before offering the necessary aid. Money became in increasingly short supply as the effects of the Black Death of 1348–9 and the accompanying bad harvests made themselves felt. Roughly one third of the population died of the plague, and as the available labour grew less, so the demand for higher wages grew more. But the war had heightened a spirit of nationalism that was reflected in the vernacular poems of Chaucer and Langland, and in 1362 the King's speech in parliament was for the first time made in English.

In 1369 – a bad year for Edward – his 'most dear consort Philippa' died and the French war resumed. Bertrand du Guesclin, the able new leader of the French forces, devastated the English army while Edward's eldest son earned the title of 'Black Prince' by his cruel sack of Limoges. By 1375 Edward was forced to sign the Treaty of Bruges which left England with only Calais, Bordeaux and Bayonne.

The following year the Black Prince died and Edward, prematurely aged, sadly declined. The King's second surviving son, John of Gaunt, assumed control of the government. Edward lived just long enough to celebrate fifty years on the throne. The chronicler Walsingham wrote that 'during the King's last illness that shameless harlot, Alice Perrers, continually spoke to him of those pleasures to which he was most attached, neither caring for the continued welfare of his soul herself nor permitting others to do so . . . until, noting his voice fail, his eyes grow dim and the natural warmth leave his body, the infamous jade tore the rings from his fingers and departed.' Edward was buried in Westminster Abbey beside Philippa, his Queen.

Manuscript

Edward III

(right, with King David II of Scotland, left)

Painting   Westminster Abbey

Richard II

53

Richard II 1377–1399

Much was expected of the eleven-year-old boy who succeeded Edward III. Through his father, the Black Prince, who was enormously popular in England, and his mother Joan, 'the fair maid of Kent', he inherited both French and English royal blood. Richard became an exceptionally cultivated and intelligent king, but his true character remains something of an enigma. On the one hand he could be weak and unbalanced, subject to uncontrollable outbursts of childish temper, while on the other he is the statesman, the lover of peace, art and literature, patron of Froissart, Chaucer and Langland and founder of the first art school in England.

He was quite striking in appearance, with auburn hair and blue eyes, and meticulous and extravagant in his dress.

Most historians would agree that Richard ruled in very difficult circumstances, and although he lacked tact in dealing with his barons, they invariably lacked loyalty and integrity in their dealings with him. During his minority the King suffered much from his overbearing uncles, particularly the domineering Duke of Gloucester. These were years of increasing discontent amongst the peasants. Matters came to a head in 1380 with the crushing poll-tax, mainly to pay for the costly war with France. Led by Wat Tyler and Jack Straw, the peasants marched to London where John Ball, 'the mad priest of Kent' addressed them on the theme:

> *When Adam delved and Eve span*
> *Who was then the gentleman ?*

The crowd was unruly, and when during a meeting with the fourteen-year-old King and his retinue Wat Tyler was killed by one of the King's men, a nasty riot was avoided by Richard who called to the crowd, 'I will be your leader and captain. Follow me to the fields and I will grant your demands.' The peasants dispersed but terrible reprisals were exacted in the name of the powerless King. In this climate the ideas of John Wycliffe spread rapidly through his 'poor preachers' in spite of their persecution, and their followers became known as 'Lollards' because of the way they 'lolled' or mumbled their prayers.

The hangings stopped the following year at the request of Anne of Bohemia, who arrived in England to marry the King. Richard and his subjects became devoted to her, and Chaucer dedicated his *Legend of Good Women* to Anne. Richard leaned more towards a small group of cultured friends than to the barons, who, under Gloucester, formed a powerful group known as the Lords Appellant. They were unable, however, to prevent Richard quietly assuming control of the government a year later when he was twenty-three. For eight years Richard ruled wisely and peacefully. He showed originality and independence by making a truce with Scotland and trying to solve the problem of absentee landowners in Ireland.

When Anne of Bohemia died childless in 1394 Richard's character deteriorated. He was distracted with grief and never returned to the Manor of Sheen where she died. Two years later, he entered into a diplomatic marriage with the King of France's seven-year-old daughter, thus calling a halt to the French wars. Richard's personal rule now became increasingly despotic. He felt that parliament was encroaching on his authority and claimed that the law of England was in the King's own mouth. He suddenly turned on the Lords Appellant and tried them for their former conduct. The Earl of Arundel was beheaded, the Earl of Warwick banished and the Duke of Gloucester murdered at Calais. Richard's cousin, Henry of Bolingbroke, Earl of Derby and Duke of Hereford, was banished in 1398 over a quarrel with the Duke of Norfolk. The King became ever more unpopular, and by thus exiling a member of the royal family he created a focus for malcontents abroad. Richard crowned this act of folly by taking the Lancastrian estates when Bolingbroke's father, John of Gaunt, died.

In July 1399, while Richard was in Ireland, Henry Bolingbroke came to claim his inheritance, landing at Ravenspur in Yorkshire, where many barons joined him. Richard returned to England and took refuge in Conway Castle, but he was tricked into the open, and forced to abdicate. A parliament was called to accept the abdication document and offer the throne to Bolingbroke. Richard was sent to Pontefract where the rigours of winter and the harsh treatment he received probably hastened his death in February 1400, although rumours spread that he had been starved. Richard was eventually buried beside his Queen in Westminster Abbey. He was only thirty-four when he died.

Henry IV 1399–1413

Henry Bolingbroke, now proclaimed King as Henry IV, had declared when he turned Richard from the throne 'that the realm was nearly undone for default of governaunce and undoing of the good laws', and amid considerable enthusiasm the Archbishop of Canterbury set him upon the empty throne. Thus did a Prince of Lancaster assume the crown, as Gower put it, 'by right of conquest, by right of inheritance and by popular election.' But Henry was well aware that he had won the crown through might and the gift of parliament, and that what had been given could be taken away; thus he was careful to stress his hereditary right, ignoring the fact that his second cousin, Edmund Mortimer, had a better claim than he had. 'Uneasy lies the head that wears a crown,' he says in Shakespeare's play, and aware that he stood in slippery places he rather ostentatiously showed himself the most constitutional of sovereigns, whilst ensuring that Edmund Mortimer, Earl of March, was kept in custody.

In many ways Henry was the complete antithesis of his cousin Richard. Where Richard was tall, attractive and frail, Henry was short, stocky and an excellent soldier. Whereas Richard was a firm believer in absolute monarchy, Henry was supple and pliant, ready to compromise if self-interest dictated it, and anxious to secure the Church as a useful ally even if it led him into a policy of persecution. His coronation had been hurried on, and perhaps to add solemnity to his person, the story was spread abroad that the holy oil used for his anointing had been confided by the Blessed Virgin Mary to St Thomas of Canterbury for the hallowing of a King who should win back the land lost by his ancestors and drive the infidel before him. He solemnly instituted the Order of the Bath, with his four sons amongst its first members. This was probably partly an attempt to throw a cloak of legality over the new monarchy and to provide champions for its defence.

The King was always chronically short of money, and the necessity of the crown was parliament's opportunity. The House of Commons greatly enlarged its powers in 1401 when it secured a recognition of the principals of freedom of debate, and three years later asserted the principle that members should be free from arrest. Both parliament and the Church were concerned at the spread of Lollard ideas, such as stripping the Church of its wealth. The wealthy laity felt uneasily that similar arguments could be applied to them, and in 1401 the first anti-heresy statute, *De Heretico Comburendo*, became law. That same year William Sawtry, a Lollard priest, was burned at the stake.

'The unquiet times of Henry IV' were troubled with rebellions. The French King and some of his own barons supported the claim of Edmund Mortimer; the Scots were causing trouble on the border and the Welsh under Owen Glendower were making a bid for freedom. In 1403 Harry Percy, known as Hotspur, son of the Earl of Northumberland, captured the Scottish Earl of Douglas at the battle of Homildon Hill. When Henry ordered him to hand over his prisoner Hotspur made common cause with Glendower. Captors and captives together plotted to take over the country. They confronted Henry at Shrewsbury and in the ensuing slaughter Hotspur was killed, and the cries of 'St George and Victory!' prevailed over the shouts of 'Esperance, Percy!'. The old Earl of Northumberland conspired against Henry again two years later with Richard Scrope, the Archbishop of York, and Thomas Mowbray, Earl of Nottingham. Henry captured and executed Mowbray and Scrope, and Northumberland fled to Scotland, only to be killed in 1408 at the battle of Bramham Moor.

After the death of his first wife, Mary de Bohun, by whom he had four sons and two daughters, Henry married Joan, daughter of Charles the Bad, King of Navarre, in 1402. The marriage was very unpopular as it was rumoured that Joan was involved in necromancy. She was in fact accused of witchcraft in 1419 and quietly confined to do penance for the rest of her life. She and Henry had no children. After the execution of Scrope, the King was afflicted with a serious illness. His contemporaries said it was leprosy, for he was troubled with unsightly eruptions on his skin and epileptic fits. Many believed that this was divine retribution for the Archbishop's violent end. The King became increasingly withdrawn and was upset by constant quarrels with his eldest son, who seemed to delight in opposing his father's policies and ministers. In March 1413, Henry was unexpectedly seized with a fit in Westminster Abbey and was carried to the Jerusalem Chamber. He was buried in Canterbury Cathedral.

Tomb effigy   Canterbury Cathedral

Henry IV

58

Henry V

Henry V 1413–1422

Most modern historians are sceptical of the chronicler who wrote that Henry 'was in his youth a diligent follower of idle practices, much given to instruments of music, and fired with the torches of Venus herself.' From the age of fourteen Henry was engaged in fighting Owen Glendower and when sixteen he commanded the English forces at the battle of Shrewsbury in 1403. He gained valuable administrative experience as Constable of Dover in 1409 and as Captain of Calais a year later, also presiding over the Privy Council when his father was ill. Policy disagreements led to his dismissal from the Council in 1412, but he succeeded to the throne a year later with many attributes of the ideal medieval king and little sign of the dissolute Prince Hal immortalized by Shakespeare. The chronicler Thomas of Elmham wrote in his life of Henry: 'The most serene prince . . . was neither of unseemly Titan size nor stunted in poor, pigmy-like shortness. He was very well-favoured, his neck was wide, his body graceful, his limbs not over-muscled. . . . He outstripped all his equals in age at running and jumping . . . in so much that, with two chosen companions, he frequently, by sheer speed of running . . . killed the swiftest fallow deer driven out in to the plain from the woodland shades.' Henry was a pious man convinced of the rightness of his own beliefs, and un-bending. When he was twenty-three he watched the burning of a Lollard and offered him a pension if he would recant. The man refused and Henry personally supervized his return to the flames. In 1414 he ruthlessly suppressed a Lollard uprising led by an old friend, Sir John Oldcastle.

Both sides in the French civil war were keen to enlist the support of the new King of England, but Henry was only prepared to assist whichever side would acknowledge him as King of France. The Burgundians were ready to support Henry, so preparations for war began. National sentiment was with the King, and his barons proclaimed that 'the King will attempt nothing that is not to the glory of God . . . if he goes to war the cause will be the renewal of his rights, not his own wilfulness.' After a series of diplomatic exchanges with France during which Henry made outrageous demands on the mad King Charles VI, an English army of twenty thousand men sailed for France on 11 August 1415. In six weeks Henry had besieged and taken the Norman port of Harfleur, but lost over half of his men in the process, mainly from disease. The rest he forced to march towards Calais until their way was blocked at Agincourt by a French army four times as big. It had been raining for days and the ground was soft and muddy, particularly unsuited to the heavy French cavalry. The battle was fought on 25 October, St Crispin's Day, and in the space of three hours the English had won an astonishing victory, marred only by the panic slaughter of most of the prisoners, including the flower of the French nobility, when Henry mistakenly thought an attempt was being made to rescue them.

In five astonishing years Henry went from one triumph to the next, and in May 1420 he achieved his French objective in the Treaty of Troyes. The Dauphin was disinherited in favour of his sister Catherine of Valois, whom Henry married, and Henry was made Regent of France during the lifetime of Charles VI, and on his death would become King. Henry spent his honeymoon capturing a few more castles, and then took his bride home to England. Henry's occupation of France was merely military and thus subject to the fortunes of war. He had foolishly allowed the Dauphin to remain at liberty, enabling him to raise troops and strike back in Henry's absence. In 1421 a combined French and Scottish army under the Dauphin defeated and killed the Duke of Clarence, Henry's brother and Commander-in-Chief in France, at the battle of Beaugé. When the Pope in Rome heard the news he exclaimed: 'Ha! The Scots are the only antidote to the English.'

Henry returned to France and spent many months driving the Dauphin and his followers across the Loire. During the siege, Henry heard the news that the Queen had given birth to a son on 6 December 1421. Henry, however, was annoyed that the child had been born at Windsor, for he had been told by his astrologers that the stars were against a confinement at Windsor, and several chroniclers mention that Henry prophesied disaster in store for his son. The long winter siege took its toll on Henry's health. Already prematurely aged through living a hard soldier's life, he became seriously ill, and having calmly arranged his affairs, he died at the Castle of Vincennes on 31 August 1422 with Catherine at his side. He never saw his son. His body was brought back to England and buried in Westminster Abbey.

61

Henry VI 1422–1461

Woe to the land where the King is a child.

Henry VI at nine months was the first baby to inherit the throne of England. Some say he remained a baby all his life, while others maintain that the gentle, pious King had an intelligence and sensitivity at odds with his time. Henry lacked the necessary ruthlessness, political skill and military prowess to cope with the crippling inheritance of Henry V and the aftermath of a long minority. John Blacman, Henry's chaplain, described the King as 'a simple man, without any crook or craft or untruth . . . with none did he deal craftily, nor ever would say an untrue word to any.' Henry also dressed very plainly, 'rejecting expressly all curious fashion of clothing.' Many stories are told of the King's preference for learning and religious devotion to affairs of state. By the time he was twenty Henry was already planning a new school at Windsor and a new college at Cambridge. All his life he took an intense interest in both institutions and left minute details for the completion of the buildings in his will.

Charles VI of France died within months of Henry's succession and the infant King of England at the age of one was proclaimed King of France also. The Dauphin was stationed at Bourges and his supporters referred to him as Charles VII, but their cause made little headway against the English forces under John, Duke of Bedford, Henry's uncle. Another uncle, Humphrey, Duke of Gloucester, governed England while the King put in the occasional appearance at such functions as the opening of parliament, where he 'schriked, cryed and sprang' during the ceremony. Henry's education was entrusted to Richard, Earl of Warwick.

Henry was apparently deprived of his French kingdom by divine intervention. 'Before Joan came,' declared one French General, 'two hundred English could beat five hundred French; but now two hundred French could beat five hundred English.' Whether or not Joan of Arc was sent by God, or carefully trained by some French nobleman, she put new life into the timid Dauphin and rallied the entire French nation to her

Painting   *National Portrait Gallery*

Henry VI

63

standard. Within five months of seeking out the Dauphin she had driven the English from Orléans and organized Charles' coronation at Rheims. In spite of the trial and burning of Joan as a witch by the English in 1431, the tide had turned, and in eighteen years the Hundred Years War was over. The English had nothing left in France but Calais.

In 1445 Henry had married the fiery and tempestuous Margaret of Anjou. She was quite unable to keep out of politics and allied with the powerful Beaufort family against the Duke of Gloucester and his cousin, Richard, Duke of York. As the English position in France deteriorated, so did the conduct of domestic affairs. In 1447 Gloucester was murdered, and in 1450 Jack Cade, an ex-soldier, led an abortive rebellion to express widespread discontent with the government. When in 1453 the French war was lost, Henry went mad. Richard of York, the heir-presumptive, was appointed Protector, but Margaret gave birth to a son, Edward, a few months later, and York found himself deprived of a peaceful succession.

By December 1454 Henry had made a complete recovery. Margaret now looked on York as a deadly rival and forced Henry to dismiss him. York and his powerful supporter, Richard Neville, Earl of Warwick, immediately took up arms and defeated the royalist forces at the battle of St Albans in May 1455. This marked the beginning of the Wars of the Roses between the adherents of the House of Lancaster, symbolized by the red rose, and the House of York, symbolized by the white rose. The fighting was to drag on spasmodically for the next thirty years. Richard of York now openly claimed the throne, but was killed at the battle of Wakefield in 1460. His head wearing a paper crown was presented to Margaret of Anjou, but his cause was continued by his son Edward, who was proclaimed King in London after winning the second battle of St Albans in 1461. The Lancastrian forces were again defeated at Towton a few months later, and Margaret and Henry fled to Scotland. But Margaret refused to give in. More troops were raised and set against the Yorkists. In 1464 Henry was captured and kept in the Tower of London until the Earl of Warwick, now known as the king-maker, briefly expelled Edward and reinstated Henry. In 1471 Edward again seized the throne, murdered Henry's son, and sent Henry back to the Tower where he, too, was murdered on 21 May. His enemies reported that he had died 'of pure displeasure and melancholy', but according to tradition Henry was killed while at prayer. A marble tablet marks the spot in the Tower of London and every year on 21 May white lilies from Eton and white roses from King's College, Cambridge are placed there. He is buried at Windsor.

Edward IV 1461–1483

In 1461 Edward's position was precarious. He was only nineteen and well aware that he had only reached the throne through the support of the Earl of Warwick, the richest and most powerful man in England. Margaret and Henry were still at large and in the spring of 1464 they raised forces against him in Northumberland, but were defeated. Margaret and her son escaped but Henry was captured and imprisoned in the Tower of London while numerous Lancastrian knights and nobles were put to death. Edward now felt ready to shake off the oppressive guiding hand of Warwick. The first clash arose over his marriage. Tall and good looking, Edward had the charm and polish associated more with an Italian merchant than an English prince and he was inclined, as the French chronicler Commynes put it, 'to think of nothing but upon women, and that more than reason would.' Edward met and fell in love with a Lancastrian widow, Elizabeth Woodville, a former maid-of-honour to Margaret of Anjou. She refused to become the King's mistress and for five months their marriage remained a secret while Warwick planned a dynastic alliance for Edward in France. The inevitable revelation angered and humiliated the Earl, as did the ennoblement of Elizabeth Woodville's family, for which eight new peerages were created. Warwick complained that the King 'resolutely maketh more honourable account of new upstart gentlemen than of the ancient houses of the nobility.' Edward refused to allow his brother the Duke of Clarence to marry Warwick's daughter Isabella, whereupon Warwick and Clarence went to France to plan a rebellion.

For three years bloody exchanges turned and overturned the fortunes of the Yorkist and Lancastrian factions, and notable was Warwick's realignment with the Lancastrian side in a reconciliation with the intrepid Margaret and her husband Henry VI. In 1470 Edward was chased out of England, and took refuge with Charles the Bold of Burgundy.

In 1471 he returned, defeated and killed Warwick at Barnet in April. At Tewkesbury Margaret was captured, her son done to death, Henry imprisoned and soon murdered. King Edward's brother, 'false, fleeting, perjured Clarence', was later charged with treason and drowned in a butt of malmsey wine.

Having effectively removed all serious opposition, Edward's authority was never again seriously threatened, and he made a studied appeal to the mercantile classes, particularly the London merchants, by an economic policy which was designed to protect English industry and trade and keep out cheap imported goods. He realized that much of the anarchy of recent years had been due to the chronic poverty of the crown and he was determined he would be as wealthy as possible. He demanded benevolences for the higher clergy and got them, and he protected the interests of the traders and artisans and all to whom peace and good order mattered most. By developing his own financial resources he avoided the dependence on parliament which had dogged the Lancastrians. He had a shrewd head for business and engaged profitably in the wool trade. In 1475 at Picquigny in France he extorted a handsome pension from King Louis in return for keeping out of French affairs. Although he kept a splendid court and had extravagant tastes, Edward was the first English king for many years to die free of debt. The administration of justice was also tightened up and Edward personally approved the introduction of torture by John Tiptoft, Earl of Worcester, the curious paradox who was also a humanist and book collector. Edward, too, took a great interest in the new learning and encouraged William Caxton in setting up his printing press. Like his contemporaries in Renaissance Italy, Edward kept his ear to the ground and it is said that he had a spy in every government department. He was described by the chronicler John Hardyng as 'a goodly man of personage, of stature high, of countenance and beauty comely, of sight quick, broad breasted and well set, in every other part comfortable; of a pregnant wit, of stomach stout, and high courage.'

Edward died unexpectedly on 9 April 1483, after a short illness. No good reason has been given for his death but several of his contemporary chroniclers put it down to the result of promiscuous living. He was buried with great ceremony in Westminster Abbey. The fifteenth century political writer John Fortescue wrote of Edward, 'I blissed be oure Lord God for that he hath sent Kyng Edward the IV to reign upon us. He hath don more for us than ever did kyng of Ingland.'

Edward IV

67

Edward V 1483

Edward V had been born in the sanctuary of Westminster Abbey during his father's temporary exile, and when called to the throne he was only twelve years old. When his father died in 1483, Edward was at Ludlow Castle on the Welsh border in the care of his uncles, Earl Rivers and Lord Richard Grey. The King's death had come so suddenly that no proper provision had been made for a long minority, and the old nobility viewed the Queen's Woodville relatives with loathing and distrust. When Queen Elizabeth wrote to her brother at Ludlow telling him to bring Edward immediately to London with a large escort, many of the nobles saw this as an indication that the Woodvilles intended to secure the Regency. Edward IV had appointed his younger brother, Richard Duke of Gloucester, as his son's guardian, but he was in the north when he received the news of the King's death. He put his retinue into deep mourning, had prayers said for his brother's soul and proclaimed Edward V as King. He then set out for the south with the Duke of Buckingham.

The events of Edward V's three month's reign are impossible to set out objectively nearly five hundred years after the event when no unbiased contemporary version exists. The confusion begins with the meeting of the two groups journeying to London at the end of April 1483. When Edward reached Stony Stratford with his uncles, news came to them that Richard and Buckingham were ten miles away in Northampton. Lord Rivers and Sir Richard Grey left Edward and set out to meet the party from the north. Apparently after meeting on friendly terms, Rivers and Grey were accused of 'trying to set distance' between the King and his uncle of Gloucester. They were arrested and sent under armed guard to Pontefract. Very few of Edward's actions are on record, but it is reported that when Richard informed him that his mother's relatives were plotting to seize the government, he wept. On 1 May the Queen heard of the arrests and immediately took sanctuary in Westminster Abbey. At that time any church was regarded as a sanctuary or holy place, where no one, not even a criminal, could be touched. The Queen took with her her younger son Richard, Duke of York, and her daughters, and is quoted as saying, 'a woe worth him! For it is he that goeth about to destroy me and my blood.' Most historians assume she was referring to Richard of Gloucester.

On 4 May Richard and Edward entered London, and Richard was proclaimed Protector and Defensor of the realm. Edward took up residence in the Tower of London and plans were set in motion for his coronation on 22 June. On 10 June Richard sent to his estates in Yorkshire for aid against the Woodvilles who, he claimed, were conspiring to destroy him and the Duke of Buckingham. On 16 June Richard frightened Elizabeth into sending the young Duke of York to join his brother in the Tower to keep him company. Shortly after this, Richard claimed that he was approached by John Stillington, Bishop of Bath and Wells, who told him that he had performed a marriage ceremony between Edward IV and Lady Eleanor Butler, and that only the three of them had been present. Several contemporaries, including Commynes and the Chronicler of Croyland, mention this episode which in any event is impossible to prove. On 22 June Dr Ralph Shaw gave a sermon at St Paul's Cross in London based on the text, 'Bastard slips shall not take deep root.' He announced that Edward IV had contracted a bigamous marriage with Elizabeth Woodville and that their children were therefore illegitimate, leaving Richard of Gloucester as the rightful heir to the throne. On 25 June parliament petitioned Richard to accept the crown and his coronation was fixed for 6 July.

Nothing more was publicly seen or heard of Edward V and his brother. Even before Richard's coronation rumours started circulating about the fate of the princes. According to the Tudor historian Holinshed, upon whom Shakespeare based his play, Richard tried in vain to persuade Sir Robert Brackenbury, Governor of the Tower, to murder the boys. Richard then prevailed upon Sir James Tyrrel, the Master of the Horse, to steal into the princes' bedchamber and smother them. Tyrrel is said to have confessed to the crime while in the custody of Henry VII for quite another offence. In 1674 the bones of two young boys were found buried under a staircase in the Tower and were accepted by Charles II at the time as those of the princes. The skeletons were re-buried in Henry VII's chapel in Westminster Abbey with an inscription blaming their murder on Richard. Whatever did happen to the boys, they were under the protection of Richard III at the time of their disappearance, so inevitably he will always be associated with their deaths.

Manuscript   Lambeth Palace

Edward V
(right, between King Edward IV and Elizabeth Woodville)

RICARDVS · III · ANG · REX ·

Painting

National Portrait Gallery

Richard III

71

Richard III 1483–1485

Thomas More, one of the most respected men in English history, has described Richard III as 'little of stature, ill-featured of limbs, crook-backed, his left shoulder much higher than his right, hard favoured of visage and such as is in princes called warlike, in other men otherwise. He was malicious, wrathful, envious and, from before his birth, ever froward. It is for truth reported that the Duchess, his mother, had much ado in her travail that she could not be delivered of him uncut, and that he came into the world with the feet forward – as men be borne out of it – and (as the fame runs) also not untoothed.' But from as early as 1603 writers have come forward to rebut this view of Richard. Men such as William Winstanley, who wrote in 1684 that 'this worthy Prince's fame [hath] been blasted by malicious traducers, who like Shakespeare in his play of him, render him dreadfully black in his actions, a monster of nature rather than a man of admirable parts.' The defence of Richard III has since become a cause for which the main protagonists are the Fellowship of the White Boar (Richard's emblem) in Britain and the Friends of Richard III in the United States. The truth about Richard III must lie somewhere between these two extremes, as it is most unlikely that anyone could be quite as evil as the Richard portrayed in Shakespeare's play, and yet, in contemporary terms, few men could be quite so self-less and noble in their motives as Richard's posthumous friends maintain he was.

In the early years of Edward IV's reign, when the King was surrounded by treachery and intrigue, the one man who had remained constantly loyal to him was his brother Richard. There are many contemporary descriptions of Richard but none mentions any physical deformity. In fact it seems that Richard was not unlike his handsome elder brother, but much slighter in stature and less self-indulgent by nature. The Countess of Desmond when an old woman remembered Richard as a young man and said, 'he was the handsomest man in the room except his brother Edward, and was very well made.' Richard accompanied his brother to the Low Countries in 1470 during his brief exile, and so distinguished himself at the battles of Barnet and Tewkesbury that Edward made him Constable of England. Through his wife Anne, younger daughter of the Earl of Warwick, he inherited vast estates in the north and it seems that the King deliberately built up his brother's power and authority, perhaps to offset that of the Woodville faction. In 1480 Richard was made Lieutenant General in the north and his administration of the area earned him widespread popularity.

Like most of the nobility, Richard feared and disliked the Woodvilles, and the measures he took to prevent a Woodville-dominated minority when Edward died clearly would have had strong support. His actions in proclaiming his nephews illegitimate and claiming the throne for himself are scarcely open to good interpretation, but it could well be, as A. R. Myers argues, that 'if he could have prolonged his reign to twenty years instead of two, he might have overlaid with success and good deeds the memory of his path to the throne.' For Richard proved to be a capable and energetic ruler, carrying on policies established by Edward IV.

Four months after his accession Richard dealt successfully with a rebellion led by his former ally the Duke of Buckingham to put forward a Lancastrian claimant to the throne. The man they had in mind was Henry Tudor, the great-grandson of an illegitimate son of Edward III, who had lived in exile in Brittany since the battle of Tewkesbury in 1471. Richard's position became weaker when his only legitimate son, Edward, died in April 1484 at the age of ten, and when his wife Anne died the following year of tuberculosis. The evidence indicates that Richard was very fond of Anne and would hardly have contrived her death, as Tudor historians maintain, to marry his niece Elizabeth, sister of the murdered princes.

On 7 August 1485 Henry Tudor landed at Milford Haven in Wales with about two thousand French troops, and marched to meet Richard at Bosworth near Leicester. Richard's army was twice as big as Henry's but he was betrayed at a crucial moment of the battle by Lord Stanley, who alone commanded more men than Henry. The battle lasted two hours with neither side losing more than one hundred lives. Richard refused to flee and died 'fighting manfully in the thickest press of his enemies', crying, 'I will not budge a foot, I will die King of England.' His body was stripped of its valuable armour and carried naked into Leicester flung across a horse. He was buried at the Grey Friars Church there but the grave was destroyed at the dissolution of the monastries under Henry VIII and his remains were cast into the River Soar.

Henry VII 1485–1509

When the battle of Bosworth was over, Richard III's coronet was found in a hawthorn bush and placed on Henry Tudor's head by Lord Stanley. Thenceforth, the Tudors assumed as a device a crown in a bush of fruited hawthorn. Henry progressed from Bosworth to London, and as he entered the Tower he was accompanied by the nobles riding two to a horse to demonstrate their new-found unity. The twenty-eight-year old Henry was crowned in Westminster Abbey on 30 October by the Archbishop of Canterbury, and a parliament summoned in November was informed by Henry that 'he had come to the throne by just title of inheritance and by the sure judgement of God, who had given him the victory over his enemies in the field.' Henry's hereditary right was weak. He was descended from John of Gaunt and his mistress Catherine Swynford, but he had won the crown through his own enterprise and luck at Bosworth and was resolved to keep it by his own prudence. He eliminated the young Earl of Warwick, who had a direct Plantagenet claim to the throne, and a few weeks after his coronation, Henry married Elizabeth of York, sister of the murdered princes, thus joining the rival houses of York and Lancaster. To commemorate the union Henry created the red and white Tudor rose which he had carved on the wall of St George's Chapel, Windsor.

Henry VII was a shrewd man. He realized the value of good public relations and made a cult of St George, the patron saint of England. He named his eldest son Arthur after the popular hero of the Round Table, and commissioned the Italian Humanist, Polydore Vergil, to write a history of England. Vergil described his patron as 'remarkably attractive and his face was cheerful, especially when speaking; his eyes were small and blue, his teeth few, poor and blackish; his hair was thin and white, his complexion sallow.' Henry dedicated himself with great tenacity of purpose and outstanding ability to pacify England, to repair the ravages of civil war and firmly to establish himself and his family on the throne. In all this he succeeded in spite of the occasional rebellion and tumult. He

Painting by Michael Sittow

National Portrait Gallery

Henry VII

crushed all pretenders to the throne; Lambert Simnel, the baker's son who pretended to be the Earl of Warwick, ended up working in the royal kitchens, and Perkin Warbeck, who pretended to be Richard of York, the younger of the two princes who died in the Tower, was executed. Henry further secured his position by important dynastic marriages. He played Spain off against France by marrying his son Arthur to Katherine of Aragon, daughter of Ferdinand and Isabella. When Arthur died a few months after the wedding in 1501, Henry, not wanting to lose the dowry or the Spanish alliance, secured a papal dispensation for Katherine to become betrothed to his younger son Henry. In 1503 Henry's daughter Margaret married James IV of Scotland, a marriage that was later to unite the crowns of Scotland and England.

Henry created a Committee of the Privy Council, and in the pursuit of justice named the Court of the Star Chamber to deal with 'compassings, imaginations and confederacies'; it became the busiest and most formidable law-court in the kingdom. Henry preferred to fine rebels rather than execute them, and like Edward IV sought money from enforced loans rather than ask parliament for a grant. His Chancellor, Archbishop Morton, worked on the principle that if a man lived poorly, his money must have been hidden away and if he lived extravagantly he obviously had plenty – a stratagem known as 'Morton's Fork'. But the country in general thrived under Henry. By judicious treaties he helped stimulate trade, and by building new cargo vessels he diverted much of the carrying trade away from the Venetians and the Hanseatic League.

Although Henry was personally a man of frugal tastes he realized the value of ritual to the monarchy. He set up a personal retinue, the Yeoman of the Guard, the first permanent military force in England, albeit a small one. It was their duty to search the straw of the King's large four-poster bed with a dagger to make certain 'that there be no untruth therein'.

Henry suffered in middle age from gout and chest complaints, and died in 1509 at the age of fifty-four, at his magnificent palace of Richmond. He was buried in the superb chapel he had built on to Westminster Abbey, the outstanding architectural monument of a prosperous age.

Henry's deliberate policy of achieving power in Europe without conflict gained for him the reputation of having brought the Middle Ages to an end and laid the foundation of modern society based on trade and law. His efficient if merciless fund-raising machinery created for him royal wealth on a scale never before dreamed of in Britain. This miserly man left his country a safer and richer place. Yet it is hard to like him.

Henry VIII 1509–1547

History has been kind to Henry. Remarkably well remembered as a free and easy, jovial, self-indulgent playboy, his vindictiveness and cruel nature are tacitly accepted as inevitable to his role as absolute monarch. Mounting the throne at the age of eighteen, he was to rule for nearly forty years.

Henry VIII saw himself as the epitome of the great Renaissance prince, the kingly equivalent of a Leonardo da Vinci. The Venetian Ambassador wrote a glowing account of the King to his masters in which he said that 'nature could not have done more for him. He is much handsomer than any other sovereign in Christendom; a great deal handsomer than the King of France; very fair, and his whole frame admirably proportioned. On hearing that Francis I wore a beard he allowed his own to grow; and as it is reddish he has now got a beard that looks like gold. He is very accomplished; a good musician; composes well; is a capital horseman; a fine jouster; speaks good French, Latin and Spanish; is very religious. . . . He is extremely fond of tennis, at which game it is the prettiest thing in the world to see him play, his fair skin glowing through a shirt of the finest texture.' Henry created an irresistible and magnificent court around himself, luring great painters, like Holbein, great musicians, like the Bessanos, and great writers such as Erasmus to England. Six weeks after his coronation Henry married Katherine, his brother Arthur's popular and pious widow. She too was called a 'miracle of learning' but was shocked at the wild behaviour of the courtiers at the feasting, dancing, masques and tournaments in which the King delighted. After the quiet restraint of Henry VII his son did everything on an astonishingly grand scale and had it proclaimed by the time he was twenty-five that as a King he had 'no superior on earth'.

Behind the glittering court lay the day-to-day administration of the kingdom. The evidence indicates that Henry found the detail of such business boring, that he was not a brilliant statesman nor an initiator. These things he left to others. Henry excelled in the way he chose and used

77

people to work for him. He was ably and loyally served by some outstanding men, but when they let him down they were ruthlessly disposed of. Cardinal Wolsey engineered the greatest spectacular of the Renaissance at the meeting between Henry and Francis I of France at the Field of the Cloth of Gold, but had to go when he failed to get a divorce for Henry from Katherine so that the King could marry Anne Boleyn. His first wife Katherine had suffered numerous miscarriages, still-births and short-lived sickly children, and her only surviving child was a daughter, Mary, born in 1516. Being only the second generation of his line on the throne, Henry was desperate for a male heir. To gain his divorce he put a quiet conscience and the national interest before obedience to Rome and declared himself Head of the Church of England in 1534, but he continued to use the title of *Fidei Defensor* conferred on him by the Pope a few years earlier. Henry's Chancellor, the saintly Thomas More, had no illusions about the outcome of the King's 'Great Matter', and when his daughter told him that the new Queen Anne did nothing but dance, he replied, 'Alas poor soul, her dances will knock our heads off like footballs; but ere long her head will dance the like dance.' From the beginning of his reign Henry had shown no qualms about 'managed' state trials. He showed an increasing vindictiveness about dispatching those who angered him, whether they be adulterous wives like Anne Boleyn and Catherine Howard, old friends like Thomas More or old servants like Thomas Cromwell.

Henry banked on the great gulf that had grown up between the clergy and laity and met with little opposition in creating the national Church and dissolving the monasteries. Ironically his six wives left him with but three children – two girls and a boy. The reason for this was not Divine disfavour, as Henry thought, but probably the venereal disease he con-tracted when he was a young man.

As Henry grew older he became grotesquely fat and suffered agonies from the weeping ulcers on his leg. Towards the end, his weight made him physically helpless and he had to be moved with the aid of machinery and numerous attendants. He became increasingly irrational, dangerous and bad-tempered. He died on 27 January 1547. Two weeks later his body was taken in solemn procession to Syon House on the way to its final resting place at Windsor. When the coffin was placed in the chapel it burst open and 'all the pavement of the church was with the fat and the corrupt and putrefied blood foully imbued.' What remained of Henry was buried beside Jane Seymour in St George's Chapel, Windsor.

Henry VIII

Edward VI 1547–1553

The news of the old King's death was suppressed for three days, but not because there were any fears for the succession of the nine-year-old heir to the throne. As long as one of Henry's children lived there was no question of any other family ruling England, for Henry VII had laid the foundations which Henry VIII had built upon to make a new style of monarchy. The King was no longer addressed as 'Your Grace' but as 'Your Majesty', and the loyalty and devotion that had been due to an over-lord in the past was now given to the country, and the Tudor monarchy embodied a national pride.

In his will Henry had left power mainly in the hands of a Council of Regency. During those three stolen days Edward's uncle, Edward Seymour, manoeuvered himself into a position of strength. The Council offered Seymour the Protectorship of the realm and the Dukedom of Somerset, and for the next two years he ruled like a king.

Henry had left instructions in his will that Edward was to be married to Mary, Queen of Scots, his sister Margaret's grandaughter. The chances of this match seemed remote, especially as the French King was making overtures to the Scots on behalf of his own son. With tact and diplomacy Somerset might have achieved something, but instead he set out to force the issue and beat the Scots at Pinkie near Edinburgh on Saturday 10 September, a day since known in Scotland as 'Black Saturday'. Not surprisingly the Scots objected to 'the manner of the wooing' and sent their six-year-old Queen to France.

Throughout 1548 there were demonstrations of social discontent and religious confusion. Vast numbers of ex-monks and nuns were looking for work at a time when jobs were already short and inflation was high because of constant debasement of the coinage. Somerset showed genuine, if ineffectual, concern for the poor and also repealed the repressive religious legislation of Henry's later years, as well as the old 1414 Act for the Burning of Heretics. But the Protector was not above filling his own

Painting, studio of William Scrots   *National Portrait Gallery*

Edward VI

81

pockets from the spoils of the dissolution of the chantries in 1547, and he built a fine palace for himself in London called Somerset House. Many of the poorly-paid chantry priests had earned extra money by teaching, and a great debate has since arisen over whether the famous Edward VI grammar schools were new foundations or old schools with new names. But the trend was certainly, if slowly, to set up new schools for those who could afford them.

In January 1549 Somerset executed his brother Thomas Seymour for treason. He had been too friendly with the Princess Elizabeth, and had tried to turn the King against the Protector by slipping him extra pocket money and encouraging him to complain to the Council about the Protector. There was already a faction waiting in the wings for Somerset's downfall, headed by John Dudley, Earl of Warwick. By October Somerset had lost the support of the Council, and the new regime epitomized Thomas More's definition of government as 'a conspiracy of rich men procuring their own commodities under the name and title of a commonwealth.' In January 1552 Somerset was executed, having been charged with planning an insurrection. Edward VI, who was then fourteen, coolly wrote in his diary that 'the Duke of Somerset had his head cut off upon Tower Hill between 8 and 9 o'clock this morning.'

The portrait of Edward painted in 1550 gives a picture of the boy's character as well as his frail physique. Precocious and intelligent, fanatically religious, melancholy and morbid, he was educated by Protestant scholars such as Roger Ascham. By the age of thirteen he could read Aristotle in Greek and translate Cicero. His meticulous diary, 1549–1552, should give us an insight into the boy's mind, but it is strangely impersonal and cold.

Edward suffered from deafness and weak eyes, and by 1553 it was clear that he had consumption and would not live long. Dudley, now Duke of Northumberland, stood to lose everything with the King's death for, according to Henry VIII's will, Edward was to be succeeded by Mary. Northumberland persuaded the King to make his own will, excluding both Mary and Elizabeth from the throne, and appointing Lady Jane Grey, the granddaughter of Henry VIII's sister Mary, as heir to the throne. Shortly before the will was drafted Northumberland had arranged a marriage between his son Guildford Dudley and Lady Jane Grey. Edward's last recorded words were instructions to Archbishop Cranmer to sign the will. He died on 6 July aged fifteen and was buried in Henry VII's chapel in Westminster Abbey.

Jane Grey 1553

Lady Jane Grey was fifteen years old when she was caught up in the net of Northumberland's intrigues. When Edward died in 1553 the only Tudors left were women. The legal heir to the throne was Princess Mary, but Northumberland had persuaded the King that he could make a will passing over his sisters Mary and Elizabeth and his cousin Mary Queen of Scots in favour of another cousin, Lady Jane Grey. Strictly speaking it was Jane's mother Frances who should have been nominated, but as she was already married to the Duke of Suffolk she did not suit Northumberland's purpose. Lady Jane was very intelligent, very Protestant and very pious, and was persuaded by Northumberland and her ambitious parents that it was her duty to accept the crown and prevent it from falling into the hands of the Catholics. A few weeks before Edward died, Jane had been married to Northumberland's son Guildford Dudley at Durham House in the Strand, and so when Jane was escorted to the Tower and proclaimed Queen on 10 July, Northumberland's son went with her.

If the Earl had been able to kidnap Mary Tudor his ambitious project might have succeeded, but she had ignored the summons to her brother's death-bed and retreated to Framlingham in Suffolk, convenient for an escape across the Channel if need be. The Council sent her an insulting order to submit to Queen Jane which she treated with contempt, and had herself proclaimed Queen. There was a general air of confusion and uncertainty, but Mary found herself gaining popular support. The Council prevailed on Northumberland to lead a force against Mary. He left London reluctantly on 13 July not trusting his fellow conspirators, and as he went he remarked to Jane's father, who had come to see him off, 'The people press to see us but not one saith, God speed.' He had not been away long before the Council gave way to arguments from the Earl of Arundel and threats from the Earl of Pembroke, who told them, 'If my lord of Arundel's persuasion cannot prevail with you, either this sword shall make Mary Queen, or I shall die in her cause.' Northumberland was

Lady Jane Grey

84

abandoned and Mary proclaimed Queen on 19 July. Lady Jane's nine-day reign was over and she left the Tower with obvious relief and returned to Syon House, protesting that she had never wanted to be Queen in the first place.

Northumberland and his dwindling army had retreated to Cambridge where he staked everything on a complete *volte face* by denouncing Jane and throwing his cap in the air in honour of Mary. He was arrested and escorted to the Tower where, to the horror of the Protestant party, he professed that he had always been a Catholic at heart. He wrote to a friend from prison, 'An old proverb there is, and that most true – a living dog is better than a dead lion. Oh, that it would please her good grace to give me life – yea, the life of a dog.' Northumberland was executed on 22 August, and Lady Jane commented to a friend, 'I pray God, I, nor no friend of mine die so. Should I, who am young and in my few years, forsake my faith for the love of life? Nay, God forbid!'

Mary refused to execute Lady Jane and wrote to her cousin, the Holy Roman Emperor Charles V, that although Jane had been condemned to death, 'she could not find in her heart or conscience to put to death her unfortunate kinswoman, who had not even been an accomplice of Northumberland but merely an unresisting instrument in his hands.' Mary showed remarkable clemency to the conspirators, but when Jane's family became involved in an insurrection led by Sir Thomas Wyatt in 1554, the Queen was persuaded that her throne could never be safe so long as Jane remained alive as a focus of disaffection. Mary offered Jane the chance to spend a short time with her husband before they were both executed, but Jane refused, saying they would be together within a few hours in heaven. After seeing Guildford Dudley's headless corpse brought back from the scaffold on 12 February 1554, Jane was herself taken to the block, 'her countenance nothing abashed, neither her eyes anything moistened with tears.' She admitted the unlawfulness of her consent to occupy the throne and met her death with a calm and dignity in contrast to those others, including her father, who lost their heads trying to crown hers. She was buried beside Guildford Dudley in the Tower church of St Peter ad Vincula.

Mary I 1553–1558

Few English sovereigns have been greeted with such scenes of rejoicing as greeted Mary when she rode into London in July 1553. Mary had had a long, hard wait for this moment, and to express her joy at reaching the throne she ordered eighteen pence to be distributed to every poor householder in the City. The Queen was now thirty-seven, and from the age of twelve she had witnessed the long-drawn-out agony of her mother's divorce, had been declared a bastard, driven from Court and sent to Hatfield to act as Lady-in-Waiting to her younger sister Elizabeth, Anne Boleyn's daughter. Under Edward VI she had been subjected to every humiliation until her cousin, the Holy Roman Emperor Charles V, had threatened Edward with war if she was not left alone.

A clear picture of Mary's physical appearance was given by the Venetian Ambassador in one of his dispatches of 1554: 'She is of low stature, with a red and white complexion and very thin; her eyes are white and large, and her hair reddish; her face is round, with a nose rather low and wide; and were not her age on the decline, she might be called handsome rather than the contrary. . . . She seems to delight above all in arraying herself elegantly and magnificently.' Beneath the outward display of sovereignty, Mary wore a religious habit.

In spite of her past experiences she was not a vengeful or vindictive person, but her isolation had made her socially and politically guileless. Her court, although splendid, was hailed as 'a school of virtue, a nursery of purity, a mansion of piety'. Mary lacked Elizabeth's fine intellect but she was cool and courageous in a crisis. In particular she had the Tudor determination and a belief in the rightness of her own actions.

Mary's first parliament in October 1553 repealed the religious legislation of Edward's reign and replaced the more prominent Protestant bishops with Catholics. Mary's popularity held fast, however, until word got out that she intended to marry Philip of Spain, son of the Holy Roman Emperor Charles V. The people of Tudor England distrusted all foreigners in general and Spaniards in particular. Mary resented any objections and on 31 October 1553 she vowed to marry Philip and no one but Philip. Opposition to the match came to a head early in 1554 with Sir Thomas Wyatt's rebellion which he claimed was to prevent England 'from over-running with foreigners'. Several of her council and even her sister Elizabeth were implicated in the rebellion, but Mary stood firm and told her subjects to ignore the rebels 'and fear them not, for I assure you I fear them nothing at all.' On 25 July 1554 she married Philip in Winchester Cathedral, and in the following November the Papal Legate absolved the country from the sin of its twenty-year break with Rome.

At the beginning of 1555 the heresy laws were revived and Protestants who refused to recant were punished. About two hundred and eighty of them were burned, including Archbishop Cranmer, Bishops Latimer and Ridley. Latimer, old and sick, spoke imperishable words as he mounted the stake: 'We shall this day light such a candle in England, by God's grace, as I trust shall never be put out.' The religious persecution alienated many of her subjects from the Queen, particularly in London. Although capital punishment for quite minor offences was common at this time, there was a lot of bitterness at the burning of ordinary people who had done nothing but hold what had until recently been official doctrine.

Mary's marriage to Philip had brought her neither love nor children. He was eleven years younger than the Queen and cool and indifferent towards her. Mary was suffering from dropsy, which causes swellings in the body through fluid retention. When in 1555 these symptoms appeared the poor Queen thought she was pregnant. She went to Hampton Court for her confinement, but after a false report of the birth of a prince, it soon became obvious that the Queen was seriously ill. The prospect of a child had kept Philip in England but he seized the opportunity afforded by his father's retirement in the autumn to leave the country. The grief-stricken Queen only saw her husband once more when, in 1556, he came to persuade her to involve England in a war against France to serve Spanish interests. The loss of Calais in January 1558, which the Queen declared men would find graven on her heart, was a blow from which she never rallied.

Ten months later the unhappy and disillusioned Queen was dead, having named Elizabeth as her heir at the last possible moment. The Bishop of Winchester preaching at her funeral in Westminster Abbey reminded the court of her compassion to the poor, but the good things Mary did were overshadowed by the religious persecutions of her reign, for which the Queen became known by the name of 'Bloody Mary'.

ANNO DNI 1 5 4

LADI MARI DOVGHTER TO
THE MOST VERTVOVS PRINCE
KINGE HENRI THE EIGHT

THE AGE OF XXVIII YERES

Painting by Master John   *National Portrait Gallery*

Mary I

Elizabeth I

Elizabeth I 1558–1603

Mary had come to London when she was sure of the throne, but on 17 November 1558 Elizabeth sat in Hatfield House and waited for London to come to her. Within two days thousands had flocked to Hertfordshire, including the Council, and Elizabeth was proclaimed Queen at her own gates. This was the beginning of an emotional relationship between Elizabeth and England that was to last until her death forty-five years later.

Elizabeth was twenty-five in 1558 and was an unusual and fascinating woman. She was cultured and intelligent, and like her father enjoyed discussion and argument. In her teens it was said that 'her sweet tongue could speak distinctly Greek, Latin, Tuscan, Spanish, French and Dutch'. Like her father too, she was strong-willed and bad-tempered. 'When she smiled,' wrote her godson John Harrington, 'it was pure sunshine but anon came a storm from a sudden gathering of clouds and the thunder fell in wondrous manner on all alike.' From her mother Elizabeth inherited her vanity, her love of extravagant clothes and especially her delight in flirtation. Striking rather than beautiful, the Queen had great vitality and wit. She dangled her eligibility before the princes of Europe and her sex-appeal before the men at court. Even in old age Elizabeth liked men to dance attendance upon her, and when in 1592 she discovered that Sir Walter Raleigh had secretly married she threw him into the Tower. But the Queen, although she enjoyed the game, never yielded the prize to anyone and deliberately cultivated the image of herself as the golden virgin queen whose feeling for her country was so great she could never marry a mere man. Like an actress playing a part, Elizabeth accumulated a vast wardrobe of richly coloured, jewel-encrusted dresses 'We princes,' she said, 'are set as it were upon stages in the sight and view of all the world.' The Queen frequently took her show on the road and probably slept in more beds around England than any other monarch. The cost of these royal progresses was borne by the unfortunate nobles – economical for the Queen and breath-taking for the majority of her subjects.

The Queen appointed Sir William Cecil as Secretary of State, with the words, 'This judgement I have of you that you will not be corrupted with any manner of gifts, and that you will be faithful to the State.' Cecil, as Lord Burghley, was to serve her so well for the next forty years that the Victorian historian James Anthony Froude wrote that he 'was the solitary author of Elizabeth's and England's greatness.' But the woman who emerges from the numerous paintings, poems, books, plays and letters of the time does not give the impression of having been a puppet Queen. On the contrary she seems to have been a woman who had the knack of getting others to do things, often great things, for her, and signs of independent action were frequently checked. Sir John Hayward wrote an astonishing account of the Queen giving an audience, when 'her eye was set upon one, her ear listened to another, her judgement ran upon a third, to a fourth she addressed her speech.'

Elizabeth's main problem when she came to the throne was the religious question. Both Catholics and Protestants made overtures to her, but a Catholic settlement would have been almost impossible in view of her birth. Elizabeth herself held no strong views on religion and boasted that she 'made no windows into men's souls'. 'There is only one Jesus Christ,' she said, 'and all the rest is a dispute over trifles.' She reinstated the Church of England and made herself Governor. The Pope eventually retaliated with the Bull *Regnans in Excelsis* in 1570, but it was too late to affect the course of events other than to harden popular opinion against Rome. The Jesuits who came secretly to serve the Catholics in England were inevitably portrayed as part of the endless plotting against the Queen emanating from Philip of Spain and Mary Queen of Scots, who had been in Elizabeth's custody since 1568. Elizabeth's government became increasingly severe on Catholics, religious persecution began again, and in 1587 Elizabeth reluctantly agreed to the execution of her cousin Mary Queen of Scots, muttering to herself, '*ne feriare feri*' – 'strike lest thou be stricken.'

The following year came the blow that Elizabeth had anticipated and feared for many years. In July 1588 Philip II of Spain launched his 'invincible Armada' against the nation which had never wanted him as King, had rejected his religion and whose pirates had for years attacked his ships and colonies overseas. Spain had gained extensive lands in the New World across the Atlantic from which English traders were excluded. They retaliated by forcing their way into Spanish colonial ports or intercepting Spanish treasure ships returning from America. Men such as Francis Drake, Walter Raleigh and John Hawkins became heroes, and were frequently rewarded in secret for their exploits against the Spaniards.

Philip naïvely expected the English Catholics to rise on his behalf, but the country was united in adversity. Elizabeth went to Tilbury and told her soldiers, 'I am come among you, as you see, at this time, not for my recreation and disport, but being resolved, in the midst and heat of the battle, to live and die amongst you all . . . I know that I have the body of a weak and feeble woman, but I have the heart and stomach of a King, and of a King of England, too; and I think foul scorn that Parma, or Spain, or any prince of Europe should dare to invade the borders of my realm.' The crescent-shaped Armada was sighted off the Cornish coast on 19 July. Francis Drake finished his game of bowls at Plymouth Hoe and embarked on a ten-day harassment of the seven-mile long Spanish fleet. The new streamlined English vessels, the use of deadly fire-ships and the 'Protestant gale' all combined to defeat the Spaniards and 'pluck their feathers little by little'.

The next fifteen years saw the full flowering of the Elizabethan Renaissance – the poetry of Edmund Spenser, the music of Orlando Gibbons and William Byrd, and above all the drama of Christopher Marlowe, Ben Jonson and William Shakespeare. Elizabeth herself attended the first performance of *A Comedy of Errors* and *A Midsummer Night's Dream*. The same exuberant spirit can be seen in the men involved in the expansion of Elizabethan England. English seamen challenged Spanish dominion overseas. In 1579 Francis Drake claimed California, while in 1584 Walter Raleigh set off with a charter from the Queen to explore and colonize the West Indies and the south coast of America, to which he gave the name Virginia. Richard Hakluyt boasted that the English, 'in searching the most opposite corners and quarters of the world . . . have excelled all the nations and peoples of the earth.'

Elizabeth kept something of her aura to the end, despite her grotesque appearance in old age. She wore a huge, spangled red wig and where she had lost her front teeth, stuffed layers of cloth under her lips to fill out her face. In the last weeks of her life, suffering from a chill, she sank into a deep depression. Robert Cecil, Burghley's son, urged her, 'Your Majesty, to content the people you must go to bed.' 'Little man, little man,' she answered, 'is *must* a word to use to princes?' She died in the early hours of the morning on 24 March 1603 in her seventieth year. She was buried in the same vault as Mary Tudor in Henry VII's Chapel in Westminster Abbey.

Painting by Daniel Mytens   *National Portrait Gallery*

James I

James I 1603–1625

With Elizabeth's death the Tudor line ran dry. James VI of Scotland was descended from Henry VIII's sister Margaret, and he became James I of England. It had been a long, tense wait as no one could be sure that the old Queen would not try to alter the succession at the last moment. James was now thirty-seven and only too delighted to get away from the poverty and strictures of the Scottish court, but he had to send to London for the necessary funds for the journey. By the time he reached London three months later he is said to have created two hundred and fifty new knights.

The first Stuart King has been described as the comic offspring of the lovely Mary Queen of Scots and Lord Darnley, and he certainly struck his new subjects as something of an oddity. He was a plain man and his hard Scottish upbringing had given him a strong accent – and such a terror of being stabbed that he wore quilted and padded clothes which made him waddle like a duck. Although coarse-minded and ungainly in his habits, he was a tough and clever man with a high opinion of his own abilities. He was very well-read and wrote extensively himself on such subjects as witchcraft, in which he believed, smoking, in which he did not, and kingship, which he revelled in. He clung inflexibly to the doctrine of the Divine Right of Kings, and he did not understand the relationship between the English monarchy and parliament. He once told the Spanish Ambassador, 'The House of Commons is a body without a head. The members give their opinions in a disorderly manner. At their meetings nothing is heard but cries, shouts and confusion. I am surprised that my ancestors should even have permitted such an institution to come into existence. I am a stranger and found it here when I arrived, so that I am obliged to put up with what I cannot get rid of.'

Parliament did actually come very near to being 'got rid of' on 5 November 1605. James was due to open a new session that day but a plot was discovered to blow up the House of Lords. Guy Fawkes was arrested in a cellar which was found to contain thirty barrels of gunpowder. He confessed that he and four other Catholics had planned to put James' daughter Elizabeth on the throne and blow the Scots back to Scotland. The conspirators were hunted down and executed, and there was such a backlash against Catholics that some Catholic historians have suggested that no plot ever existed, and that the government invented it to discredit the Catholics.

James disliked Puritans as much as he disliked Catholics, and told them clearly at the religious conference at Hampton Court in 1604: 'No bishop, no King.' The Puritans felt themselves increasingly at odds with the established Church and a group of them went to Leyden in Holland in 1608, but were less than happy there. They thought of 'some of those vast and unpeopled countries of America, which are fruitful and fit for habitation', and obtained permission from the King to settle there. On 6 September 1620 a group of Puritans from Leyden and the West Country left Plymouth in the *Mayflower* and landed at Cape Cod Bay in America, where they founded another Plymouth, and have been known ever since as the 'Pilgrim Fathers'.

James' relationship with parliament grew steadily worse. Inflation, his own extravagance and his disastrous foreign policy made him dependent on parliamentary grants, which were often refused without redress of grievances. James reversed Elizabethan policy towards Spain, first by trying to marry his son Charles to the Infanta, and later by sacrificing Sir Walter Raleigh to propitiate Spanish anger. There was an outburst of criticism in parliament in 1621. The King unwisely tried to silence the members, but the Commons replied by inserting in their journals a sober protestation of their privilege to speak freely on all subjects of debate. James sent for the book and tore out the offending leaf with his own hand. One of the weaknesses of the King's position was his extravagant and licentious court: 'a continued masquerado, where the Queen and her ladies . . . appeared often in various dresses to the ravishment of the beholders.' James' Queen, Anne of Denmark, was a great patron of the arts. She had a beautiful palace built at Greenwich by Inigo Jones. She and James quarrelled constantly, and after her death in 1619, the King never remarried. He was a homosexual and had no interest in women. Most influential of his male favourites was George Villiers, whom he made Duke of Buckingham.

Dubbed the wisest fool in Christendom, James died of a stroke in 1625, and was buried in Westminster Abbey. His best gift to the nation was his sponsorship of the new translation of the Bible – the Authorized Version.

Charles I 1625–1649

The twenty-four-year old King presented a striking contrast to his father. He was slightly built, fine-featured, dignified and refined, with cultivated artistic tastes. He was the patron of Rubens and Van Dyck and made an unrivalled collection of paintings. He had been very frail as a child, and though he outgrew his physical defects and made himself a fine horseman, he always suffered from a slight impediment of speech which made him present a chilling reserve to all but his wife and the Duke of Buckingham. He was always slow in speech and action, and had a habit of postponing or shirking the settlement of a difficulty, and when he did act he too often gave the impression that he was playing a double game. His greatest weakness was that he was a bad judge of men and women. In the early years of his reign he was too much influenced by his father's old friend the Duke of Buckingham.

Buckingham's mismanagement of foreign affairs involved England in wars with France and Spain for which parliament refused to grant supplies without impeaching the Duke. Charles retaliated by dissolving parliament. It was said that 'Charles placed him in the balance against the whole nation.' A paper nailed to a post in the city asked: 'Who rules the kingdom? The King. Who rules the King? The Duke. Who rules the Duke? The Devil. Let the Duke look to it.' When the King was told the news of Buckingham's assassination on 23 August 1628 he was in church, but 'continued unmoved and without the least change of countenance till prayers were ended.' He then rushed off in hysterics.

Charles married Henrietta Maria, the daughter of Henry VI of France, by proxy on 1 May 1625 when she was only fifteen. He ordered a temporary suspension of the persecution of Catholics, thereby deceiving his wife, who wanted permanent toleration, and parliament which wanted none. After three stormy years James and his Queen became quite devoted to each other, but Henrietta Maria was an intriguing meddlesome woman and ill-fitted to help or guide her husband.

Painting by Daniel Mytens   National Portrait Gallery

Charles I

97

Up to 1629 the domestic history of Charles' reign is a disagreeable tale of bickering with parliament over religion, money and the disputed exercise of the royal prerogative. Charles believed in the Divine Right of Kings, and had a very legalistic mind: once convinced of the technical merit of his case he went ahead, as one modern historian puts it, 'inflexibly trampling over the susceptibilities, religious or economic, of his people'. After a furious row with the Commons in March 1629, Charles dissolved parliament and ruled without it for the next eleven years. During this period the King enjoyed a false sense of security, delighting in his family and his patronage of the arts, but this peaceful period came to an abrupt end when the Scots refused to accept an anti-Puritan prayer book. Charles tried to crush the rebellious Scots, but his weak forces were not strong enough and he was forced to call the Short and then the Long Parliament. From the outset the King met with determined opposition. The crisis came early in 1642 when Charles, urged on by Henrietta Maria, foolishly tried to arrest five members of parliament. Never before had a monarch entered the House of Commons. In July the King raised his standard in Nottingham.

The civil war lasted four years, and was won by parliament, with its superior armed forces and longer purse. The Queen had fled to France, but Charles was in custody on the Isle of Wight and his captors could not agree on what to do with him. In January 1649 the Rump Parliament created a special court to try the King for being 'a tyrant, a traitor, a murderer and public enemy.' Charles refused to recognize the authority of the court. The end was inevitable but magnificent. Whatever mistakes Charles had made during his life he made up for in the courage and dignity with which he faced death. When the executioner asked for the customary pardon before raising the axe, the King replied, 'I forgive no subject of mine who comes deliberately to shed my blood.' Charles' last words were, 'I go from a corruptible to an incorruptible crown, where no disturbance can be, no disturbance in the world.' He was buried in St George's Chapel, Windsor.

Commonwealth 1649–1659

Oliver Cromwell, Lord Protector
1654–1658

Oliver Cromwell was a Squire, born in Huntingdon and educated in strict puritan beliefs first by his tutor and then at the University of Cambridge, which towards the end of Charles I's reign was a stronghold of puritanism. He made plans to emigrate with his family to New England, but came instead to represent Cambridge in the Long and the Short Parliament. Sir Philip Warwick noted in 1640 that he was 'very ordinarily apparelled, for it was a plain-cloth suit, which seemed to have been made by an ill country tailor: his linen was plain and not very clean . . . his voice sharp and untunable and his eloquence full of fervour . . . he was very much harkened unto.'

When war broke out Cromwell joined the Earl of Essex, the Leader of the parliament troops, with sixty horse. At the battle of Edge Hill in 1642 he observed the inferiority of the parliamentarian to the Royalist cavalry, and Cromwell determined on that field to recruit a body of cavalry to fight for parliament which should be better led, better armed and better disciplined. Returning to the eastern shires he raised a cavalry force of 'honest, godly men', trained under strict military discipline. 'Swearing, dicing, wenching' were all severely punished, and he succeeded in imparting his own fiery religious zeal to his troops. At the battle of Marston Moor in 1644, Cromwell commanded the new force and he routed the King's cavalry, earning the nickname which was later applied to all his troops – Ironsides.

But the winning of the war was the least difficult of his tasks. In one of his sonnets Milton addresses these words to Cromwell: 'Peace hath her victories no less renowned than war', and it was these victories of peace that were to escape Cromwell's grasp. After the execution of the King, England was declared a 'Commonwealth' and Cromwell tried to govern through the Rump Parliament. He went to Ireland to suppress a Royalist uprising, and his violent slaughter of the garrison and townsfolk at Drogheda and Wexford are a terrible stain on his character, seeming still more frightful through his own protestations that 'this is a righteous judgement of God upon these barbarous wretches.' He went on to Scotland and in 1653 pursued a Royalist army south to Worcester and defeated it. Cromwell returned to London to find parliament unpopular, unrepresentative and unwilling to dissolve itself. In April 1653 Cromwell's troops cleared the Commons, and he tossed the Speaker's mace after the departing members, shouting, 'What shall we do with this bauble?' That night someone scribbled on the door of the Commons: 'This House to let – unfurnished.'

Cromwell replaced the Rump with a group of hand-picked Puritans who came to be known as the Barebones Parliament, but this was dissolved too after a few months. In 1654 a group of army leaders drew up a written 'Instrument of Government' and Cromwell was invested with the title of Lord Protector. On 4 April he and his family moved into the Palace of Whitehall.

In February 1657 parliament offered Cromwell the crown, and when he refused, a new constitution made him King in all but name. He was to be called 'Your Highness' and allowed to appoint his own successor. Cromwell was already prematurely aged. His constant fear of assassination made him neurotic about travelling or sleeping in the same room two nights in a row. He died of a fever on 3 September 1658 and was buried at Westminster Abbey. At the restoration, however, his body was dug up and hanged on a gibbet at Tyburn, and his head placed on a pole at Westminster Hall. His body was later reburied at Tyburn and his head taken to his old college, Sidney Sussex, at Cambridge.

Cromwell is a baffling character. He is one of the greatest cavalry leaders in history, yet he had never been on a field of battle until he was forty-three years of age. With resolution, vigour and clear-sight he combined deep religious zeal and conviction. In an age of religious fanaticism he was, however, tolerant, extending a clemency rare in that age to both Jews and Quakers. The picture of him as a soured ascetic is inaccurate. He was exceedingly fond of horses and hunting, a lover of music and art, and he kept statues in his Hampton Court garden which scandalized the strict Puritans. Far from being a 'Roundhead', his portraits show that he wore his hair long like any Royalist. He had a real enthusiasm for education, founding a university at Durham which was suppressed at the Restoration. His foreign and imperial policy both rested on a passionate desire to make England respected and feared abroad, and wars against Holland and Spain were both brought to a victorious conclusion. Clarendon wrote: 'Cromwell's greatness at home was a mere shadow of his greatness abroad.'

Painting after Samuel Cooper   *National Portrait Gallery*

Oliver Cromwell

Inset: Painting by an unknown artist   *National Portrait Gallery*

Richard Cromwell

Richard Cromwell, Lord Protector
1658–1659

Richard Cromwell was a great disappointment. The eldest son of Oliver Cromwell and Elizabeth Bourchier, he had served in the parliamentary army, and in 1647 was admitted a member of Lincoln's Inn. He had sat in the parliament of 1654 and had succeeded his father as Chancellor of the University of Oxford. He had not, however, been in any way trained for the position that was thrust upon him by his father's death. He was solemnly called to his father's bedside and nominated his successor, but he was without military and political ambition, and constantly referred to by his father as 'indolent Dick'.

His elevation to the office of Protector was deeply resented by the officers of the New Model Army, and the more austere Puritans took offence because of his careless temperament and his indifference to religious convictions. The leaders of the army formed a strong rival faction in opposition to parliament, and when he summoned his first parliament in 1659 to vote money, bitter controversy broke out. After weeks of stormy debate, the army leaders began to plot his dismissal. He had had no wish to occupy the position of Protector, and on 25 May 1659 he communicated his submission to parliament, and retired into private life.

He looked on uninterested during the months after his dismissal, as General Monk began to move south from Scotland with an army that was to restore the authority of parliament, but he became increasingly convinced that the majority of English people were tired of constitutional experiments, and longed for a return to the monarchy. Monk organized the calling of a 'free parliament', which in turn called back the King.

In 1660 Richard Cromwell left England for France, and lived in several countries under the name of John Clarke. He returned to England in 1680 and lived quietly on his estate near Winchester until he died of senile decay in 1712.

Charles II 1660–1685

Charles arrived back in England to 'enjoy his own again' on 26 May 1660. His journey to London was one long triumph and in Whitehall, after receiving endless congratulations in the hall where his father had been condemned to death, he remarked, 'It surely must have been my own fault that I did not come before, for I have met no one today who did not protest that he always wished for my restoration.' Although only thirty, Charles had the looks and experiences of a much older man. At twelve he had fought for the Royalists; he was nineteen when his father was beheaded and at twenty he had led a Scottish army into battle and fought with great courage at Worcester. For six weeks after that he was on the run, in disguise and living rough while 'wanted' notices were posted everywhere for 'a long dark man'. At one time he hid in an oak tree as Cromwell's soldiers searched the bushes below. The oak became his favourite symbol, and when he was rebuilding parts of Windsor Castle he incorporated an oak motif in the plaster of the ceilings. From 1651 until the Restoration Charles lived a life of insecurity in Holland and France where, according to the Puritans, he indulged in 'fornication, drunkenness and adultery'.

By the time he became King, Charles had lost the chubby good looks of his teens. His face had become drawn and lined, his expression cynical and mocking. Intelligent, self-seeking and witty, he trusted nobody and nobody trusted him. One of his ministers wrote that the King 'lived with his ministers as he did with his mistresses; he used them but he was not in love with them.' His contemporaries, including Louis IX of France and William of Orange, had no great opinion of Charles. They thought him unreliable, opportunist and lazy, that he had ability but rarely used it. The King had great charm, and enormous stamina. Apart from women, he loved riding, dancing, swimming, hawking, sailing, tennis and, above all, hunting. He also loved paintings and attempted to recover some of his father's old collection. He enjoyed the flowering of the newly-restored theatre, and took a serious interest in chemistry and science, which led to

Painting, studio of John Michael Wright   *National Portrait Gallery*

Charles II

the foundation of the Royal Society and the building of the Royal Observatory at Greenwich.

The first decade of Charles' reign was a difficult one. Commercial and colonial rivalry with Holland provoked a hopelessly mis-handled war. In 1665 the Great Plague broke out, followed in 1666 by the Fire of London, which burned St Paul's Cathedral and thousands of buildings, including ninety-nine city churches. In 1667 the Dutch sailed up the Medway, sank five battleships, and towed the *Royal Charles* back to Holland. The King and his friends were chasing butterflies at the time, and Samuel Pepys of the Navy Board commented bitterly, 'They mind their pleasures and nothing else.' The 1670s saw the beginnings of a new London, much of it the creation of Sir Christopher Wren. In the secret Treaty of Dover Charles allied himself with the French against the Dutch, and also promised to restore the Roman Catholic faith in England. It is doubtful whether he ever intended to carry out this promise, but his Declaration of Indulgence to non-Anglicans caused a violent outcry, and parliament squashed the Declaration and passed the Test Act to unseat all the Roman Catholic members of the government. Anti-French and anti-Catholic feeling ran high. An Oxford crowd jostled one of the King's coaches, thinking it contained his Catholic mistress, the Duchess of Portsmouth. Nell Gwyn, who was in fact in the coach, stuck her head out of the window and cried, 'Pray good people, be civil; I am the *Protestant* whore.'

The extreme anti-Catholics in parliament, led by Shaftesbury, became discredited through being connected with the 'Popish Plot' to murder Charles and his Catholic brother James, and for the last few years of his life Charles enjoyed an upsurge of popularity. His French income and customs revenue enabled him to govern without calling parliament, and ironically he exercised more power at this time than either his father or his grandfather.

Though his marriage to the unhappy Catherine of Braganza produced no children, and Catherine returned to her native Portugal, Charles himself acknowledged thirteen illegitimate children, and ennobled many of them, together with their mothers. On 2 February 1685 Charles had a stroke. During the ensuing days he was received into the Catholic Church, blessed his illegitimate children, asked forgiveness of his childless Queen, and told his friends, 'let not poor Nellie starve.' On 6 February he apologized to those who stood by for being 'such an unconscionable time a-dying'. He was fifty-five years old, and was buried in King Henry VII's chapel in Westminster Abbey.

James II 1685–1688

James II was amazed to find his accession to the throne greeted with enthusiastic rejoicing. The Test Act of 1673 had forced him to resign his post of Lord High Admiral and go abroad, and in 1679 the Whig members of parliament had tried to have him excluded from the throne. Public opinion had gone against the extreme Protestants and Catholic James had come back to court, but when Charles died James half expected an armed rebellion in favour of his illegitimate nephew James, Duke of Monmouth. Instead he was faced with an amenable and generous parliament, and at his coronation Anglican pulpits poured forth sermons advocating doctrines of Divine Right and the duty of docile obedience to the Lord's anointed. It came thus as something of a shock when Monmouth did actually land at Lyme Regis in June to claim the throne as the people's 'beloved Protestant Duke'. Parliament stood strongly behind James and the invasion only served to strengthen his position. Monmouth's troops were routed at Sedgemoor, and Monmouth was beheaded. The country folk who had supported him were either brutally put to death at the 'Bloody Assizes' presided over by Judge Jeffreys, or sent into slavery in the West Indies. The King could have shown leniency, but he did not.

Once Monmouth's rebellion had been dealt with, James determined on a course that could only end in his undoing. The Earl of Lauderdale summed up the issue when he said that James 'loves . . . to be served in his own way, and he is as very a papist as the Pope himself, which will be his ruin.' James' 'way' was the re-establishment of absolute authority and the Catholic Church. Both aims were unacceptable. Catholicism practised in private was one thing, blatant flouting of the Test Act was another. Catholics were given senior posts in the army, the government and even in the Church of England. Oxford Colleges were turned into Catholic seminaries, and in May 1688 James caused an outcry by imprisoning the Archbishop of Canterbury and six of his bishops for not announcing his Declaration of Indulgence from the pulpit. On 10 June the Queen gave

James II

birth to a son, thus destroying the hope that on James' death the crown would pass to his Protestant daughter, Mary. It was put about by the King's enemies that the baby had been smuggled into the Palace in a warming pan, and to try to prove the story broadsheets were sold in the streets showing the route the pan had taken.

On 30 June the bishops were acquitted of seditious libel, to general rejoicing, and seven leading statesmen wrote to Mary's husband, William of Orange, inviting him to invade England and save the country's liberties. Louis XIV warned James of his danger and offered French protection, but James resented the interference and refused the offer. He never thought William would be so rash as to invade England, but he was wrong. William landed at Torbay in Devon on 5 November and marched slowly towards London. James panicked, haunted by the spectres of his father, Richard II and Henry VI. Nearly all his friends deserted him, and his daughter Anne sided with William. James tried to escape to France, dropping the Great Seal into the Thames at Lambeth, but was caught and brought back. His wife and son had managed to get to France and William made sure that James' second attempt to join them succeeded. The King had fled and left the English throne vacant for William.

James threw himself on the hospitality of Louis XIV of France, and the next year made an attempt to regain the English throne with Irish–French support at the Battle of the Boyne. He was beaten, and in contrast to the valour he had shown as a young man, apparently behaved with cowardice in the fight. He spent the rest of his life in France.

In contrast to his brother, James was neither likeable nor attractive. He was arrogant, tactless and humourless, and nicknamed Dismal Jimmy by Charles' own Nell Gwyn. Like Charles, he was a womanizer, but without the same refinement. As one of his mistresses remarked, 'We are none of us handsome, and if we had wit, he had not enough himself to discover it.' Charles had once said that his brother's mistresses were so ugly that they must have been imposed on him as a penance.

James died of cerebral hemorrhage with syphilitic inflammation of the arteries on 6 September 1701, at St Germains.

William and Mary 1689–1694
William III 1689–1702

When William was invited to England it was not assumed that he would become King, but James' flight left the throne vacant and William was there, and willing. He knew that the nobles who had invited him to England were in an awkward position. 'The English were for putting the Princess Mary singly on the throne and were for making *him* reign,' said William, referring to himself, 'by *her* courtesy. No man could esteem a woman more than he did the Princess; but he was so made that he could not hold anything by apron strings.' Mary was adamant in her refusal to rule alone and told Lord Danby 'that she was the Prince's wife and never meant to be other than in subjection to him and that she did not thank anyone for setting up for her an interest divided from that of her husband.' Parliament had no choice but to offer the crown jointly to William and Mary on 6 February 1689.

Although he was a grandson of Charles I, William was a Dutchman by birth and inclination. He had taken a great risk by invading England, and seems to have been motivated by a desire to preserve his wife's inheritance and secure English support in his wars against France. He was not an impulsive man and must have thought carefully about the venture before embarking on it, but once having decided on a course of action he always acted swiftly. He was an intelligent man but taciturn and reserved. When he became King, Lady Cavendish commented that he 'is a man of no presence, looks very homely at first sight; yet, if one looks long at him, he has something in his face both wise and good.' William concealed his feelings under a mask of almost repellent coldness, and from the outside his conduct towards his wife was bad-tempered and indifferent. Yet when she died he was beside himself with grief and immediately pensioned off his mistress in a fit of remorse. Physically, he was thin and frail and suffered from asthma all his life. He never liked Englishmen and they never liked him. But for all that, when Mary died in 1694 and James hopefully awaited a call home, nothing happened.

William III

　　　　　　　　　　　　　National Portrait Gallery

Mary II

William's position in England was not such as to make him feel at home. He was well aware that in parliament both the Whigs and the Tories accepted him as a temporary caretaker of the country's fortunes and that many of his ministers were in secret communication with St Germains. Parliamentary powers were extensively developed under William, with the 1688 Bill of Rights and the 1701 Act of Settlement. The machinery of the National Debt was devised, and the Bank of England founded in 1694, issuing new coinage in consultation with Sir Isaac Newton, Master of the Mint. Thus the modern system of finance was established which was to enable the country to pay for its wars and trans-oceanic expansion. William was also the first statesman after Cromwell to grasp the importance of England's naval position in the Mediterranean.

In 1700 the childless King of Spain died, bequeathing his throne to Philip of Anjou, a grandson of Louis XIV. The following year Louis XIV of France recognized James II's son, the 'Old Pretender', as the rightful King of England. Both events combined to enrage William – who once more engaged in power politics, organizing a Grand Alliance of Dutch, English and Germans against France. War was declared, but before the fighting had begun William was thrown when his horse tripped over a mole hill at Hampton Court. Pleurisy set in and he died a few days later on 8 March 1702. 'When the King came to die,' said Sarah Churchill, 'I felt nothing of the satisfaction which I once thought I should have had on this occasion. He was buried quietly at midnight in Westminster Abbey and the Jacobites toasted "the little gentleman in black velvet."'

Mary II 1689–1694

Mary caused great offence, when she arrived in London after her father's flight, by appearing to be quite delighted at the turn of events. 'She came into Whitehall jolly as to a wedding,' wrote Evelyn, 'seeming quite transported with joy.' He goes on to say that when William and Mary were formally offered the crown on 13 February, 'it was expected that both, especially the Princess, would have showed some reluctance . . . of assuming her father's crown, and made some apology, testifying regret; but nothing of the kind happened.' The coronation was arranged for 11 April and on that morning Mary was given an angry letter from James in which he wrote 'that hitherto he had made all fatherly excuses for what had been done, and had wholly attributed her part in the revolution to obedience to her husband; but the act of being crowned was in her power, and if she were crowned while he and the Prince of Wales were living, the curse of an outraged father would light upon her as well as of that God who has commanded duty to parents.'

Up till this point Mary and her father had been very devoted to each other and she had been very sorry to leave him eleven years earlier to go to Holland. She was only fifteen when she married William, who was twelve years older and four inches shorter than she was. She had burst into tears at her first sight of him, but within a few years she overcame her aversion to her husband and her homesickness for England and learned to love both William and his country. The one great source of unhappiness in Mary's life, apart from her childlessness, was her husband's long-standing love affair with Elizabeth Villiers, one of her ladies-in-waiting. William insisted that Elizabeth be kept on in the Queen's household, and Mary would write long and bitter letters to her sister Anne about the agonies of jealousy and humiliation she suffered. Mary made herself completely subservient to her husband, and William's grief at Mary's death shows how much he had come to rely on her.

During her six years as Queen of England, Mary reigned alone for much of the time, since William was abroad conducting his campaigns against the French, or seeing to his affairs in Holland. Although Mary was continually anxious about his safety, she ruled with remarkable intelligence and vigour without him. Her bright and gracious manner and her sturdy English patriotism earned her popularity, and she devoted a great deal of time and energy to philanthropic causes. Her chaplain wrote that 'if her husband retained his throne, it would be done by her skill and talents for governing.' And William himself acknowledged that 'though I cannot hit on the right way of pleasing England, I am confident that she will.' Her down-to-earth Protestantism won approval, although the Jacobites never let go an opportunity to poke fun at Mary and her increasing size.

The last years of her life were made unhappy by constant quarrels with her sister Anne. Mary disliked and mistrusted Anne's bosom companion Sarah Churchill, and her husband, and equally the influential Churchills disliked William, and called him Mr Caliban. When Churchill was dismissed from court because of his Jacobite leanings a breach was caused between the two sisters which never healed. Anne, too, retired from court and suffered innumerable slights from the Queen until Mary's terrible death from smallpox in December 1694. To her husband Mary left a casquet of letters including one of complaint and reproof at his unfaithfulness to her. She was buried in Westminster Abbey.

Anne 1702–1714

Anne was to be the last of the Stuarts, for of her seventeen pregnancies, only five of the babies were born alive. Of these five, only one, the Duke of Gloucester, survived infancy and he died when he was eleven. Anne was the casualty of a weakness that is inevitable in royal families: they evade natural selection. Mary Queen of Scots carried a gene causing a chemical disturbance in the blood known as porphyria. This would have spelt disaster for the average family, but sickly royal offspring tend to be coddled more than most and this gene reappeared in generation after generation, bringing an end to the Stuarts and causing havoc among the Hanoverians. But Queen Anne knew nothing of porphyria and accepted her tragedies as a punishment from God for deserting her father in his hour of need, and ignoring his plea to see that the throne went to her young half-brother, James Stuart, when William III died. Neither her ambitious confidante Sarah Churchill nor her own Protestant convictions would have allowed Anne to follow such a course of action, but nevertheless it weighed heavily on her mind. The thirty-seven-year old Queen was fat, prematurely aged and crippled with gout. She was too sick to walk at her own coronation, and was carried in a sedan chair. She was basically a homely, phlegmatic, rather dull woman, but by emphasizing her 'English heart' she struck the right note with her subjects, who called her 'Good Queen Anne', and the events of her reign were destined to make it one of the most significant in English history.

In 1683 Anne had married Prince George of Denmark, who was even duller than the Queen and just as fat, and was happiest working in his carpentry shop in Kensington Palace with a bottle at his side. Anne

Painting, studio of John Closterman *National Portrait Gallery*

Anne

115

enjoyed the fuss made of her on state occasions, but after the first few minutes found the conversational strain too great. She was over-shadowed in this respect by Sarah Churchill, Lady of the Queen's Bedchamber, a brilliant and witty woman with whom Anne had been infatuated for many years. Her ascendency over the Queen was strengthened by her husband's outstanding victories in the War of the Spanish Succession, on which William III had embarked just before his death. After the Battle of Blenheim in 1704 Anne made Churchill Duke of Marlborough, and she and Sarah rode side by side to the thanksgiving service at St Paul's Cathedral. No king's mistress had ever wielded such power as did Sarah Churchill over the Queen.

As Marlborough went from glory to glory with the battles of Ramillies, Oudenarde and Malplaquet, Sarah became too confident of her position and began to neglect the Queen, and was frequently bossy and bad-tempered with her. Anne turned for comfort and sympathy to one of her ladies-in-waiting, Abigail Hill. Abigail had been planted in the Queen's household by one of the Tory leaders, Robert Harley, in order to break the spell cast on Anne by Sarah, who was a Whig supporter. The device worked and Sarah was eventually dismissed from favour after making frightful scenes in Kensington Palace and wrecking the apartments she had occupied there. She even raged at the Queen in public on the steps of St Paul's. It was inevitable that Marlborough too should fall from favour, in spite of his great service to the country, and his letter of dismissal from the Queen was so offensive that he threw it in the fire. The rift between Anne and the Marlboroughs was never repaired.

Apart from being the last Stuart, Anne was also the last sovereign to veto an act of parliament, to preside over most Cabinet meetings and to exercise that ancient tradition of 'touching' her subjects to cure them of scrofula. She did this in competition with her half-brother, the 'Old Pretender', who had a thriving healing business going at St Germains. Like her husband George, Anne too was a heavy drinker and was often described in contemporary ballads as 'Brandy-faced Nan'.

The last year of Anne's life was bedevilled with political squabbles over the succession, with the rise of the two-party system in parliament. The Tories were trying to persuade Anne to name her step-brother James Stuart, the 'Old Pretender', as her heir, while the Whigs were busy paving the way for the Hanoverians. Anne had long wanted to make divine restitution by securing James' succession, but she never changed the Act of Settlement of 1701, by which the Electress of Hanover was named as her heir, and she died on 1 August 1714 worn out by the ravages of porphyria and gout, murmuring 'Oh, my brother! Oh, my poor brother!' She was buried in Westminster Abbey, where a wax effigy made soon after her death still stands.

George I 1714–1727

George I came slowly to his English throne. His mother had just died and as the Jacobite plan to oppose his succession had completely misfired, he took his time to settle his affairs in Hanover with characteristic meticulous care. He eventually set off for England with a huge retinue, pausing on the way for numerous receptions and speeches – the third sovereign in fifty-four years to come from across the English Channel to occupy the British throne. He arrived by boat at Greenwich in thick fog on 29 September, an unknown entity to the crowd of British aristocrats who were waiting to greet him. They were confronted with a middle-aged, pale little man with bulging blue eyes and a troup of Hanoverian friends, advisers and servants, two of whom, Mohamet and Mustapha, he had captured during a campaign in Turkey. They were all determined to profit from George's rise in the world. 'A flight of hungry Hanoverians, like so many famished vultures,' wrote the Whig Minister James Stanhope, 'fell with keen eyes and bended talons on the fruitful soil of England.' Thackeray too remarked on this aspect of the Hanoverian succession: 'The German women plundered, the German secretaries plundered, the German cooks and attendants plundered, even Mustapha and Mohamet, the German negroes had a share in the booty.' One Hanoverian who did not get her share was George's wife, Sophia Dorothea, whom he had married in 1682 and snubbed and neglected for twelve years. When he discovered that she was having an affair with Count Konigsmark he shut her up in Ahlden Castle for the rest of her life, and Konigsmark mysteriously disappeared. In place of the Queen came two middle-aged mistresses, the tall, thin Ehrengard Melusina von Schulenberg, whom he named Duchess of Kendal and the short fat Charlotte Sophia Kielmansegge, whom he made Countess of

Darlington. They were known respectively as the Maypole and the Elephant.

George was well aware that he had succeeded to the throne of his distant ancestors not because anyone particularly wanted him but because they wanted the hereditary heir, James Stuart, son of the deposed James II, even less. The failure of the Jacobite rebellion which took place in 1715, the year after George came to the throne, showed not only the weakness of the Stuart leadership but also that most of those sentimental gentlemen who raised their glasses to 'the King over the water' really wanted him to stay there.

After 1715, George's reign was one of much-needed peace, owing to the setting up in Europe of a complex web of political alliances for which the King himself and his Whig ministers worked hard and skilfully. At home the greatest crisis of the reign was the financial crash known as the South Sea Bubble. After the initial success of the South Sea Company set up by the Whig ministers Stanhope and Sunderland, a wave of crazy speculation had swept the country and all sorts of wild schemes had come into existence. Reaction and panic inevitably set in, the financial bubble burst and thousands were ruined. The situation was saved by the political genius of Robert Walpole, who had both opposed and made a fortune out of the scheme. He worked to restore public credit and confidence in the King's government and came to dominate English politics for the next twenty years. He assumed the title of Prime Minister when George gave up attending Cabinet meetings, the King preferring to discuss issues privately with his ministers and his German advisers. This change marked an important step forward in the development of modern constitutional monarchy in England.

The Cabinet's power was also increased by George's inclination in England 'to leave it to itself as much as possible and to live out of it as much as possible.' In England George had shown himself heartless, cruel and mean, and he had few friends there. He usually managed to spend six months of each year in Hanover, but instead of leaving his eldest son as Regent as was customary, he rendered him politically powerless. George and his son hated each other, and in spite of a nominal reconciliation engineered by Walpole, the Prince of Wales made no secret of the fact that he could hardly wait for his father to vacate the throne. The time came sooner than he had expected. When George set out for Hanover in June 1727, he appeared to be in remarkably good health for a man of sixty-seven. Near Osnabrück he had a stroke in his coach after eating an enormous dish of melons, and died. He was buried in his beloved Hanover.

Painting, studio of Sir Godfrey Kneller   *National Portrait Gallery*

George I

George II 1727–1760

On 14 July 1727 Robert Walpole rode to Richmond to tell the Prince of Wales that his father was dead. 'Dat is one big lie!' yelled George in his broken English. But the news was perfectly true and George was to wear that much-coveted crown for the next thirty-three years. Described by Thackeray as 'a choleric little man', George had a frightful temper and would kick his wig and coat about in rages, particularly when suffering from an attack of piles. He had three great passions in life: the army, music and his wife. He was an exceptionally brave man and was the last British sovereign to fight in battle, at Dettingen against the French in 1743. In music he shared his father's love of opera and in particular the work of George Frederick Handel, who had been George I's court musician in Hanover and had come to England to enjoy the patronage of the Hanoverian kings.

George's third passion, his wife, was also his greatest asset. He had married Caroline of Ansbach in 1705 and always loved her more than any of his mistresses. In contrast to her husband, Caroline was tall, regal and vivacious. As Princess of Wales she gathered round herself, according to Walpole, 'the most promising of the young gentlemen of the next party and the prettiest and liveliest of the young ladies.' She was highly intelligent and loved talking with the greatest scholars and writers of the day. She was particularly interested in politics and was quick to appreciate Walpole's qualities. When George became King he was loth to keep on his father's chief minister but he could not stand up to Caroline's bullying, so Walpole stayed.

Robert Walpole based his political success on his maxim: 'let sleeping dogs lie'. He aimed to avoid war, encourage trade, reduce taxes and control parliament. His policies enhanced national prosperity so that England was able to stand the tremendous financial strain of the wars that were to follow. When he retired in 1742 Walpole left Henry Pelham to cope with the War of the Austrian Succession, in which George's concern for his Electorate of

Hanover brought about a hasty peace with France, to the chagrin of many of his ministers. Pitt spoke darkly of the shrinkage of the Imperial crown under the Electorate cap. Then came the Jacobite rising of 1745, when the 'Young Pretender' Bonnie Prince Charlie marched south as far as Derby. There was panic in London and the usual fears that the Catholics meant to rise and cut everybody's throat. But the moment passed, George remarked bravely, 'Pooh! don't talk to me that stuff!' and the Scots retreated in sad disarray and suffered cruelly at Culloden for their tenacious loyalty to the House of Stuart.

The 1750s saw Britain almost continually at war. Rivalry with France reached as far as India and North America as well as flaring up in Europe in the Seven Years War. George's reign drew to a close amidst scenes of patriotic hysteria reminiscent of the great days of Marlborough. The French were beaten by Clive in India, Wolff in Canada and an Anglo-Hanoverian force at Minden. Horace Walpole wrote in 1759, 'victories came so thick that every morning we were obliged to ask what victory there was, for fear of missing one.'

In true Hanoverian style, George hated his son and heir, Frederick Prince of Wales who was, by all accounts, thoroughly unpleasant and erratic in his behaviour. The Queen had refused to allow him near her when she was dying in 1737, regarding his request as sheer hypocrisy. Frederick died in 1751 when he was forty-eight, after being hit on the head by a cricket ball. A contemporary wrote:

> Here lies Fred who was alive and is dead.
> We had rather it had been his father.

His father, who had enjoyed good health until he was seventy-seven, died suddenly on 25 October 1760 from a stroke and was buried beside Caroline in Westminster Abbey. He was succeeded by Frederick's eldest son George, aged twenty-two.

Painting by Thomas Hudson   *National Portrait Gallery*

George II

George III

George III 1760–1820

'Born and educated in this country I glory in the name of Britain,' George III told his first parliament proudly, and set himself with great dedication and a high sense of duty to be a good King. As a child his mother had called him 'rather shy and backward' but as a man he favourably impressed not only Dr Johnson but also that great critic of royalty, Horace Walpole, who wrote, 'The Sovereign does not stand in one spot with his eyes fixed royally on the ground, and dropping bits of German news. He walks about and speaks freely to everybody.' George grew up at Kew and carried on his father's work of developing the exotic botanical gardens. He made Buckingham Palace his London home and he and his Queen, Charlotte of Mecklenburg-Strelitz, went to a great deal of trouble and expense choosing fine furniture, china and paintings to adorn it. John Adams, a future President of the United States wrote in 1783 when he called at the Palace as the first American ambassador to England, 'In every apartment in the whole house the same taste, the same judgement, the same elegance, the same simplicity, without the smallest affectation, ostentation, profusion or meanness.'

In his efforts to be a good King, however, George III constantly interfered in politics. His own ideas of royal prerogative clashed with the principles of parliamentary government and cabinet solidarity which had slowly developed since the time of William and Mary. The weakness of his approach was that only men of mediocre talents and servile minds were willing to accept positions as royal yes-men. It led the King to abuse and criticize some of the most independent and able of his ministers, like the younger Pitt, whom he called a 'trumpet of sedition'.

A series of inept governments and the King's own obstinacy and rigid views led Britain into the 'no taxation without representation' row with the colonies in North America. 'I wish nothing but good,' reasoned George, who never fully grasped the issues involved, 'therefore every man who does not agree with me is a traitor and a scoundrel.' George was accused of tyranny on both sides of the Atlantic and fighting broke out in 1775. Independence was declared in 1776. Under the leadership of George Washington and after the longest war ever fought on American soil, independence was complete by 1781 with the defeat of Cornwallis' army, at Yorktown, and the United States was officially recognized at the Peace of Versailles in 1783. King George never got over the 'loss of America' and was with difficulty dissuaded from abdicating.

As he grew older the King spent more time at Kew and Windsor, where he ran three farms in the Great Park. With his wife and thirteen children 'farmer George' lived a life of unwavering regularity. 'It was early; it was kindly; it was charitable; it was frugal; it was orderly; it must have been stupid to a degree which I shudder to contemplate,' wrote Thackeray, and concluded that 'no wonder all the princes ran away from the lap of that dreary domestic virtue.' Increased age also brought on more frequent attacks of the disease which first showed itself in 1765 and which has only recently been diagnosed as porphyria. The symptoms were extreme irritability, compulsive talking and hallucinations. At the time it was thought the King was going mad, particularly when he addressed trees as ambassadors and tried to throttle his eldest son. One of his doctors thought that the gout in his foot had gone to his head. In 1789 the King quite lost touch with reality, as royalty in France trembled with the outbreak of revolution, but George recovered enough to drive Pitt from office in 1801 by refusing to allow Catholic emancipation in Ireland, and then to rejoice in 1805 at Nelson's victory at Trafalgar. But his condition worsened again and from 1811 he ceased to rule, the Prince of Wales having been made Regent.

In his sad old age the Queen once came across George kneeling on the floor in his long purple dressing gown praying aloud for her, for his family, for the nation and finally for himself. He asked that God might take the burden of his illness from him, and if not, at least to help him to accept it. When he had finished he burst into tears.

The King lived to be eighty-one and died blind and deaf on 29 January 1820 at Windsor, where he was buried.

George IV 1820–1830

The sons of George III were, according to the Duke of Wellington, 'the damn'dest millstones about the neck of any government that can be imagined.' The domestic virtues of the old King were in strong counterpoint to the amorous adventures and wild extravagances of his seven boys, the eldest of whom, George Augustus Frederick, so far outstripped the others that he was known as the Prince of Pleasure. In spite of his long-standing patronage of the Whigs in parliament, and his constant opposition to his father's ministers and policies, when Regent George IV was politically conservative and never wholeheartedly involved in politics. What he lacked in political acumen he made up for in his flair for clothes, architecture, interior design, china, furniture and elegant living. He is associated with the style known as 'Regency', and he spared no expense in the building and adorning of royal residences such as Carlton House, Buckingham Palace, the Royal Lodge at Windsor and the exotic pavilion at Brighton. He restored the Castle at Windsor, which had been started by William the Conqueror, raising the tower so that it dominated the surrounding countryside. With his favourite architect Robert Nash he built some of the most beautiful parts of London, including Carlton House Terrace, the old Regent Street, and Regent's Park. He was also a collector *par excellence* of some of the finest paintings, china, furniture, military costumes, jewellery and works of art in the world. His subjects were outraged by his incessant spending – but posterity has many reasons to be grateful to him.

George was not accustomed to denying himself anything, and when he fell in love with a Roman Catholic widow, Maria Fitzherbert, in 1784, the only way he could prevail on her to share his bed was to marry her. Although the ceremony was illegal and the Prince disclaimed it, the affair shocked the public and infuriated his father. Ten years later George III forced his son to marry Princess Caroline of Brunswick, and the Prince's private life went from bad to worse. Having taken one look at Caroline he

Unfinished painting by Sir Thomas Lawrence

National Portrait Gallery

George IV

had called for brandy, and soon maintained that she was coarse, smelly and promiscuous. According to Caroline, George was very rude to her, was drunk on their wedding night and deliberately blackened her name. She left him after two weeks, gave birth to a daughter nine months later and then went to live in Italy. When the old King finally died in 1820 Caroline returned to England to claim her rights as Queen. George immediately instituted divorce proceedings against her and for several months the country was scandalized and enthralled by the sordid details of the couple's lives. The Prime Minister prepared a Bill of Pains and Penalties which was to deprive Caroline of her title. She was looked on by some as a wronged woman, but later lost public support. When the Privy Council decreed that she should not be crowned with her husband, she made a foolish attempt to force her way into the Abbey during the coronation. To the relief of many she died two weeks later of a stomach disorder. George never married again but was consoled in his old age by stout and elderly mistresses.

Among George's most notable achievements as King were his state visits. They were to set a pattern for future sovereigns. George was a great showman and adored parading himself and dressing up. He visited Ireland and Hanover, and when in Scotland he appeared in full highland dress with pink tights to cover his legs. Unfortunately he was unable to capitalize on the unexpected success of these trips owing to his declining health and grotesque bulk. He also showed signs of his father's illness in his incessant talking and his firm but erroneous belief that he had led a murderous cavalry charge at Waterloo. In the early months of 1830 he suffered a series of strokes and died on 26 June after a blood vessel burst in his stomach.

Most of his subjects would have agreed with Horace Walpole's view that the King 'was a bad son, a bad husband, a bad father, a bad subject, a bad monarch, and a bad friend.' Yet the cultural heritage George left to the nation is perhaps greater than that bequeathed by any other sovereign. He was buried in St George's Chapel, Windsor.

George I was reckoned vile –
Viler still was George the Second
And what mortal ever heard
Any good of George the Third?
When to hell the Fourth descended
Heaven be praised, the Georges ended.

National Portrait Gallery   *William IV*   Painting by Martin Archer Shee

William IV 1830–1837

When George IV's only legitimate child, Charlotte, died in childbirth in 1817, there were no younger Hanoverians left in direct line to the throne. George's five elderly sisters were either spinsters or childless and although his six brothers had numerous offspring, not one was legitimate. In an effort to prevent the House of Hanover from becoming extinct there was a flurry of matrimonial activity amongst the royal Dukes. The first brother, Frederick, Duke of York, was now heir to the throne but had fallen out with his wife and was childless. The second brother, William, Duke of Clarence, abandoned Mrs Jourdan, his mistress of twenty years and the mother of his ten children, and after several rebuffs was accepted by Amelia Adelaide of Saxe-Meiningen. They produced in quick succession two daughters who died in infancy and still-born twins. The third brother, Edward, Duke of Kent, who had been forced to leave the army because of his brutal behaviour, gave up his French mistress of twenty-five years and married Princess Victoria of Leiningen. In 1819 they had a daughter, the future Queen Victoria. The fourth brother was Ernest, Duke of Cumberland, an unpleasant sexual pervert already married to a German Princess who was rumoured to have murdered her two previous husbands. They produced a blind son, George, three days after Victoria was born. Augustus, Duke of Sussex, the fifth brother, refused to leave his mistress Lady Cecilia Underwood, but the sixth and youngest, Adolphus, Duke of Cambridge, rushed to the altar with Princess Augusta of Hesse-Cassel. They had three children and lived in Hanover, where Adolphus became notorious for his habit of shouting at preachers in church.

As Frederick, Duke of York, had died of dropsy in 1826, it was George IV's seventy-five-year-old brother William, Duke of Clarence, who succeeded him in 1830. The reputation of the monarchy was generally low and William did little to restore it. As a young man he had served in the Navy, where he had acquired a coarse tongue and a taste for women, drink and gambling. His wife Adelaide had a remarkably improving effect on him in his old age and one observer was astonished to note on meeting the pair soon after their marriage that William 'behaved perfectly well, was civil to everybody . . . [and] . . . did not say a single indecent or improper thing.' But William and Adelaide's court seemed dowdy and dull to London Society after the lavish entertaining of George IV; Princess Lieven, the Russian Ambassador's wife, complained of the lack of intelligent conversation and wrote: 'In the evening we all sit at the round table. The King snoozes and the Queen does needle-work.'

Soon after his accession William was faced with nearly twelve months of agitation, demonstrations and rioting over the Whig government's proposed reform of the antiquated system of representation in parliament. Aristocrats such as the Duke of Wellington felt that the Reform Bill meant that the days of the English gentleman in politics were numbered. Nevertheless William continued, at times reluctantly, to back the Bill and it eventually got through the House of Lords when the King threatened 'to create such a number of peers as will be sufficient to ensure the passing of the Reform Bill'. In 1834 William again found himself involved in political controversy when he clashed with the Prime Minister, Lord Melbourne, over his Irish policy. He dismissed Melbourne – the last occasion on which a sovereign has dismissed a British Prime Minister – and invited the Tory Robert Peel to become Prime Minister. Peel found himself unable to govern with a minority in the House of Commons and resigned after one hundred days. William reluctantly reinstated Melbourne and found that he had to accept the elected government whether he liked it or not. He swore he would never dine with Whig ministers again.

In spite of his rough, blunt manner, William was regarded with a certain amount of affection, combined at times with a lack of respect bordering on contempt. When he died of pneumonia following an asthma attack in 1837, the *Spectator* wrote, 'His late Majesty, though at times a jovial and, for a king, an honest man, was a weak, ignorant, commonplace sort of person.' He was buried in St George's Chapel, Windsor. His British crown went to his niece Victoria, and the crown of Hanover, barred to women by Salic law, went to his brother Ernest, Duke of Cumberland.

Victoria 1837–1901

Princess Victoria was woken by her mother at 6 o'clock in the morning of 20 June, four hours after the death of William IV. In her long cotton dressing-gown, with her hair streaming down her back, she went downstairs to receive the homage of the Archbishop of Canterbury and the Lord Chamberlain. After the throne had been occupied successively – in the words of Sir Sidney Lea – by 'an imbecile, a profligate and a buffoon', Victoria's appearance must have seemed like a move from the ridiculous to the sublime. In her Journal that day the Queen wrote, 'I am very young and perhaps in many, though not in all things, inexperienced, but I am sure that very few have more real good will and more real desire to do what is fit and right than I have.' Victoria had been brought up like a hot-house plant by her mother, the Duchess of Kent, who was totally under the influence of Sir John Conroy, the Comptroller of her Household. The pair of them had long looked forward to the time when the Duchess would be Regent and Victoria a pliant tool in their hands. To ensure her daughter's dependence on her, the Duchess had isolated her from outside influences, had made her sleep beside her at night and had cut her off as much as possible from her Uncle William at Windsor. It was a great relief to the dying King and the new Queen that four weeks earlier Victoria had celebrated her eighteenth birthday and could therefore rule in her own right.

Victoria was small and slim, and gave the misleading impression of simplicity and frailty. In fact she enjoyed remarkably good health throughout her life and, although always honest and direct in her dealings with people, was a very complex woman. She had dignity and presence, could be as cold as iron and yet was passionate and sentimental. Many of those who knew her loved her dearly, but everybody who met her was in awe of her. She was always moved by beauty and particularly enjoyed the company of good-looking men. She was vulnerable to their flattery, and after her accession to the throne there was nearly always close to her a man

Painting by George Hayter   *Victoria*   National Portrait Gallery

133

on whom she could lean and who could influence her. Initially it was the Prime Minister Lord Melbourne, then Prince Albert, then Prime Minister Disraeli. Unfortunately for the Liberal leader Gladstone, it was never him. In her old age her servants John Brown and the Indian Karim fulfilled this role. The relationships were, of course, always very respectable and reflected Victoria's strange, fatherless childhood – the Duke of Kent had died when Victoria was a baby, and even in her relationship with Albert she still looked for a father-figure to lean on.

Victoria's husband, Prince Albert of Saxe-Coburg-Gotha, was more important to her than anything else in the world. She married him when she was twenty and was totally and utterly devoted to him. They had nine children who married into all the royal families of Europe – and through passing on the haemophiliac gene that Victoria carried, brought to an end the Russian and Spanish dynasties.

Victoria did nothing without Albert's approval, and he advised her on everything. At Osborne on the Isle of Wight he created a domestic setting that entranced her. It was Albert's initiative and enthusiasm that brought about the Great Exhibition of 1851, to celebrate the achievements of the industrial era. It was his love of art and of 'science' that led to the building of the complex of museums at South Kensington in London. But there was something humourless about the Prince Consort, with his deep-seated belief that every human being was capable of unlimited improvement if only he tried hard enough.

When Albert died of typhoid in 1861, Victoria was beside herself with grief. She slept with his night-shirt in her arms and a cast of his hand within reach. For years she retired from public life, staying at Osborne, Windsor or Balmoral. She always insisted on seeing the state papers and made her ministers come to her. She was only persuaded to emerge from this cocoon of mourning by the tact and charm of the Conservative Prime Minister, Benjamin Disraeli, and she never fully realized the dangerous unpopularity she had incurred after Albert's death. Republican sentiment was widespread and many resented paying large sums of money to a sovereign who appeared to do very little in return. On more than one occasion Victoria had the unpleasant experience of being booed, and *The Times* demanded that she 'show herself to the present generation which knows her not'. Disraeli cleverly linked Victoria with the new enthusiasm for empire-building and in 1876, in the teeth of a fair amount of opposition, secured for her the title of Empress of India. In 1887 she celebrated her Golden Jubilee, and wrote: 'All was the most perfect success'. She did not return to her old seclusion, and by the time of her Diamond Jubilee in 1897 the Queen had become the symbol of British greatness and the focus of renewed loyalty and patriotic sentiment. Compton Mackenzie wrote: 'Her Diamond Jubilee almost made the public believe that she personally during her long reign had created the British Empire.'

Although Disraeli might flatter Victoria that 'the course of a Ministry depends upon the will of the Queen', she was well aware as her reign entered the twentieth century that the government of the country was no longer directly affected by the wishes of the crown. Republicanism was no longer an issue; the nation looked to its sovereign for other qualities than those of a good Prime Minister. In Victoria these took the form of motherhood, respectability and duty. When she died of old age in 1901 there was a very definite sense of the ending of an era. Princess May lamented, 'The thought of England without the Queen is dreadful even to think of. God help us all!' Victoria was buried beside Albert in the mausoleum at Frogmore near Windsor.

Edward VII 1901–1910

Albert Edward, Duke of Cornwall, Duke of Rothesay, Earl of Carrick, Baron of Renfrew, Lord of the Isles, Great Steward of Scotland – or Bertie, as he was known to the family – was the first male heir to be born to a British monarch for nearly eighty years. By the time he was three, Queen Victoria had decided that her eldest son was dull and dreamy and she had a horror that he would turn out to be like his great-uncle George IV. She longed 'to see him resemble his angelic dearest father in every respect, both in body and mind.' She and Albert imposed a rigorous regime of study on Bertie, with very little sport or recreation. Even Walter Scott's novels were considered too trivial for the mind of a future king. From being a bright co-operative child Bertie became unruly and resentful, and when on his seventeenth birthday his father presented him with a document which began: 'Life is composed of duties', he broke down and wept. Edward only gained his independence at the age of twenty-two when he married the lovely Princess Alexandra of Denmark, whom Victoria hoped would be his salvation. She always expected the worst of Edward, and once let out of his domestic prison the Prince of Wales embarked on a career that fulfilled all her expectations.

With two homes of his own, Marlborough House in London and Sandringham in Norfolk, plus an income of £100,000 a year, the Prince spent the next forty years making up for lost time. Edward was deeply attached to Alexandra and was quite sincere when he promised his mother: 'Love and cherish her you may be sure I will to the end of my life', but in his extra-marital escapades he was greatly helped by his wife's dignified 'blind eye'. Marlborough House became the meeting place for the fastest set in London. The Prince was cited in more than one divorce case and was having affairs with other women until well into his sixties. His mistresses ranged from French chorus girls, society ladies and such Edwardian celebrities as Sarah Bernhardt and Lillie Langtry. Edward seemed to have an insatiable appetite for women, food, drink, gambling

Edward VII

and travel. Victoria was appalled and confided to her Journal, 'What will become of the poor country if I die?' Unfortunately, Victoria refused to give Edward a responsible role to play or to delegate any of her duties to him. She only grudgingly allowed him to visit India in 1875 and then resented his success.

In spite of Edward's risqué reputation and ignorance of the duties of a monarch, he was hailed with great enthusiasm as 'Good old Teddy' when he finally became King at the age of sixty. Far from allowing the solemnity of his new position to hamper his pleasures, Edward threw himself into life with renewed gusto, and yet at the same time was a remarkably conscientious King. He would often start work on the red boxes containing state papers after a late party and work into the early hours of the morning. For the first time since 1886 the sovereign opened parliament in person, and Edward made it an occasion of great pageantry and display. From his youth Edward had always been very clothes conscious, and set new trends in fashion. He popularized the Homburg hat and double-breasted coat and had his trousers ironed, nautical style, flat to the seam.

During his short reign, Edward made his greatest popular impact in the field of foreign policy. He had travelled widely in Europe visiting his numerous relatives and once he became King he was able actively to assist foreign office negotiations. His charm and tact contributed to the important *entente cordiale* between France and Britain in 1904 and the Anglo-Russian *entente* of 1907. On the domestic front, the King was horrified by women's suffrage and the proposal for legalized picketing. In particular he was concerned by the growing conflict between the government and the House of Lords. In 1909 the Chancellor of the Exchequer, Lloyd-George, presented his 'People's Budget' which proposed heavy taxes on high incomes and big landowners. The House of Lords rejected the Budget and the Prime Minister, Asquith, appealed to the country. The Liberals were returned with a reduced majority but got the Budget through. Asquith asked Edward to create more Liberal peers, effectively to reduce the power of the House of Lords. Edward refused, and in the middle of the ensuing crisis suffered a bout of bronchitis and died on 6 May after a series of heart attacks. The last news the King heard before his death was that his horse 'Witch of the Air' had won at Kempton Park races.

George V 1910–1936

George V came to the throne a shy, retiring, unknown and quite undistinguished man of forty-five. On the day of his Silver Jubilee twenty-five years later he was quite overwhelmed by the tumultuous ovations which greeted him, and remarked to the Archbishop of Canterbury, 'I am sure I cannot understand it, for after all I am only a very ordinary fellow.' But strangely enough, in a reign that encompassed political upheaval, the First World War and the Great Depression, the ordinariness, homeliness and conscientiousness of George V endeared the monarch to his subjects. They could identify with a King who was neither well read nor particularly well educated, who looked upon bridge as too 'highbrow' a game and whose favourite entertainment was the musical 'Rose Marie'.

As Edward VII's second son, George had been destined for a career in the Navy, while his older brother Prince Albert Victor was groomed for the throne. Albert, however, died of pneumonia in 1892 and George took over both his brother's position as heir to the throne and his fiancée, Princess May of Teck, whom he married in 1893. For the next seventeen years before ascending the throne, George did little else, according to his biographer Harold Nicholson, but 'kill animals and stick stamps in a stamp album'. As King, H. G. Wells complained that George's court was 'alien and uninspiring'. 'I may be uninspiring,' George replied, 'but I'll be damned if I'm an alien.' The virtues of dignity, duty, courage and hard work that he strove to embody set the pattern for the future of the monarchy in Britain, while elsewhere in Europe during George's reign, five emperors, eight kings and eighteen minor dynasties disappeared.

The years before the First World War were turbulent ones in Britain. George had become King in the midst of a constitutional crisis over the power of the House of Lords. No sooner had the peers capitulated than there were violent disturbances over the proposed Home Rule Bill for Ireland, numerous strikes by bitter, impoverished workers and demonstrations by thousands of women demanding the vote. Their cause acquired a martyr when Emily Davison threw herself under the King's horse at the Derby in 1913. When war broke out with Germany in 1914 the ranks closed against the enemy. The King gave up all alcohol for himself and his family while the fighting lasted and Queen Mary saw to it that none of the Royal Household should exceed his food ration. Both the King and Queen went to France to visit the troops, the King in the trenches and the Queen at the hospitals. On one occasion the King's horse reared, threw him and then rolled on him, breaking his pelvis. He was never without pain from the accident for the rest of his life.

After the war, economic troubles and industrial unrest reached their peak with the General Strike of 1926 and this was followed in the late twenties by the Depression. During this period the King began the custom of broadcasting a Christmas message to his people in every part of the Commonwealth. In *A King's Story*, George's eldest son Edward wrote, 'My father, with the instinctive genius of a simple man, found the means of squaring the apparent circle within the resources of his own character . . . he transformed the crown as personified by the Royal Family into a model of the traditional family virtues.'

Sadly, the genial, red-cheeked King adored as 'Grandpapa England' by his grandchildren had been a stern and distant father to his own four sons. When his friend Lord Derby suggested that he might cultivate his sons' friendship, he replied, 'My father was frightened of his mother, I was frightened of my father, and I am damned well going to see to it that my children are frightened of me.' Queen Mary too was aloof and ill at ease with her children. Communications improved as the younger sons grew up and married, but the heir to the throne Edward remained a bachelor and was growing increasingly impatient with ceremonial duties and rigid court conventions. The King was so concerned about his heir that he confided to a friend, 'After I am gone the boy will ruin himself in twelve months.'

On 6 May 1935 anxieties were put aside for a service of Thanksgiving at St Paul's Cathedral for twenty-five years of George's rule. The economy seemed to be improving and there was a quiet air of optimism in spite of the ominous policies pursued in Europe by Hitler and Mussolini. But the year of celebration took its toll on the King's health. He suffered increasingly severe attacks of bronchitis and on 17 January 1936 he wrote in his diary, 'I feel rotten.' He died three days later and was buried in St George's Chapel, Windsor.

Painting

Royal Academy

George V

Edward VIII 1936

Edward VIII was forty-one years old when he ascended the throne, the first bachelor of mature years to become King since William Rufus. He was immensely popular, with a reputation kindled as much by his war service in Flanders and his successful overseas tours as by his youthful appearance and obvious charm. In his first broadcast to his people Edward said: 'I am better known to you as Prince of Wales – as a man who, during the war and since, has had the opportunity of getting to know the people of nearly every country in the world, under all conditions and circumstances. And although I now speak to you as King, I am still that same man who has had that experience and whose constant effort it will be to continue to promote the well-being of his fellow men.' Government Ministers listened uneasily to these words, thinking of Edward's sympathy and concern for the poor and unemployed, and hoped he would not meddle.

The new King also had something of the nervous restlessness of the war generation who had lived through the Depression, saw the rise of Fascism in Europe and were swept along by the plays of Noel Coward and the songs of Ivor Novello. But beneath the apparent glamour of his life, Edward was shy, insecure and often lonely. He had never been able to get on with his father, and the relationship became more strained as Edward's younger brothers settled down and got married. Edward found an outlet for his natural exuberance and emotions in a gay social life and particularly in the company of married women. Being one of the world's most eligible bachelors, Edward's romances naturally excited a great deal of interest in the press, particularly the foreign press.

As Prince of Wales, the King had met and fallen in love with an American divorcée now married to a London stockbroker, Ernest Simpson, from whom she obtained a divorce in October 1936. There was then nothing legally preventing the sovereign from marrying Mrs Simpson, but a constitutional crisis would have arisen if he did so against his Cabinet's advice. Another problem facing the King was his position as

Head of the Church of England; a Church which would neither re-marry nor give Holy Communion to a divorced person.

In November the King visited the poor and unemployed of South Wales, and promised them, 'You may be sure that all I can do for you I will.' But within three weeks, in the face of mounting Commonwealth, parliamentary and public opposition to Mrs Simpson, Edward decided to abdicate. When he left England for the woman he loved he hoped to be able to return and serve his country in some capacity, but apart from a brief spell as Governor of the Bahamas during the war, he was never given the opportunity. Nor did he wish to live in England unless his wife was given royal status. He died on 28 May 1972 and was buried at Windsor. It was estimated that 57,000 people filed past his coffin as it lay in State. Several years later his widow, the Duchess of Windsor, told one of his biographers, 'He might have been a great King; the people loved him.'

Pastel drawing by Frank Salisbury   Collection of Lord Brownlow

Edward VIII

144

Painting by Frank Beresford   Angus District Council

George VI

George VI 1936–1952

In the midst of world-wide speculation and critical interest, George VI succeeded his brother, whom he created Duke of Windsor. Like the rest of the Royal family, George was deeply shocked by the abdication, and he wrote to Prime Minister Stanley Baldwin, 'I am new to the job but I hope that time will be allowed to me to make amends for what has happened.' One of the first problems of his reign was to persuade his brother to stop making frequent telephone calls from his exile in Austria with advice on matters of the day, much of which contradicted the advice the King was getting from his Cabinet Ministers. This was no easy task for a man who all his life had looked up to and admired – if not even envied – his older brother.

George, like Edward, had grown up with a distant and uneasy relationship with his father, although he was very like him in temperament and as King always followed his example devotedly. George had never been physically strong, was highly strung and painfully shy. As a child he developed a bad stammer which cast a shadow over his public life until, when he was thirty, he met an Australian speech therapist called Lionel Logue. Logue described George as 'a slim quiet man, with tired eyes and all the outward symptoms of the man upon whom habitual speech defect had begun to set the signs.' With the help of Logue's breathing techniques, his wife's encouragement and his own perseverance, George eventually mastered his stammer.

During the First World War, George served in the Navy and the Air Force, becoming the first member of the royal family to obtain a pilot's licence. In peace-time he had been an active President of the Industrial Welfare Society and had instituted his unexpectedly successful camps where boys from working and upper-class families mixed together on an equal footing.

In spite of the sense of panic and feeling of inexperience that overwhelmed the King at his accession, he did have one great advantage over the previous King; something that Edward had referred to as a 'matchless blessing . . . a happy home with his wife and family.' In 1923 George, then Duke of York, had married Lady Elizabeth Bowes-Lyon. She was as gay as he was shy, as charming as he was awkward and as scintillating as he was silent. The pair were supremely happy and had two daughters, Elizabeth and Margaret. This attractive royal family's obvious dedication captivated the press and the people.

Much of the fifteen years of George's reign was dominated by the Second World War and its aftermath. When England declared war on Germany in 1939, the King saw his own position as being a vital one in upholding morale and inspiring unity. With his Ministers and his war leaders he acted as his father had done during the First World War, 'to advise, to encourage and to warn.' He developed a close relationship with Winston Churchill, who acknowledged 'the gracious intimacy with which I, as First Minister, was treated.' The King and Queen tirelessly toured bombed areas and had a narrow escape themselves when Buckingham Palace was bombed. As far as they could they shared the hardships of war with their subjects. They ate austere rations off gold and silver plate and refused to move to a place of safety. Queen Elizabeth explained that 'the children can't go without me. I can't go without the King and of course the King won't go.' The King practised revolver shooting in the grounds of Buckingham Palace, and announced he was prepared to die there fighting. In 1941 he instituted and personally designed the George Cross for gallantry, a 'new mark of honour for men and women in all walks of civilian life.'

As early as 1940 the King had predicted that life would not be easy after the war. He himself was physically and emotionally drained and became frequently depressed by the political uncertainties and economic problems of the early years of peace. In 1951 he wrote to a friend that 'the incessant worries and crises through which we have to live have got me down properly.' He witnessed the birth-pangs of the Welfare State at home and the change from Empire to multi-racial Commonwealth abroad. One modern historian has written that the King worried himself into an early grave. However, it was not the strain that killed him but cancer. He died in his sleep on 6 February 1952.

Elizabeth II 1952–

When Elizabeth became Queen she was sitting in the branches of a giant fig tree in Kenya watching wild game gather round a water-hole. At the news of her father's death she and her husband returned home immediately, and the following afternoon the new Queen received the homage of her grandmother, Queen Mary, widow of George V, who had already lived through the reigns of four kings and who had helped instil in her grand-daughter her strong sense of duty, self-sacrifice and hard work.

The coronation of Elizabeth II in the summer of 1953 took on the same religious, almost mystical solemnity that had characterized her parents' coronation. In her first Christmas broadcast Elizabeth asked her subjects to 'pray that God may give me wisdom and strength to carry out the solemn promises I shall be making.' Her coronation gown was interwoven with emblems representing all the countries of the Commonwealth, and throughout her reign the Queen has seen it as her personal responsiblilty to uphold the ideals of the Commonwealth. She has described the change from Empire to Commonwealth as a 'beneficial and civilized metamorphosis', and in her numerous foreign tours she has made herself a living link between this free association of states. She is the most widely travelled Head of State in the world, and being a Royal Ambassador for Britain has given her an outlet for genuine service and shown that the crown is not merely an abstract symbol of unity. At home the Queen is careful to maintain a completely neutral attitude to politics and it seems that she gets on much better with Socialist Prime Ministers than her father ever did. She is meticulous about doing the 'Boxes' and, as both Winston Churchill and Harold Wilson found to their embarrassment, is sometimes more up to date than her Prime Minister. When he retired, Harold Wilson said, 'I shall certainly advise my successor to do his homework before his audience.'

Queen Elizabeth's personal interests and tastes are much like those of any upper-class countrywoman. She loves hunting, shooting, fishing,

walks and riding, while the great passion she shares with her mother is horse racing. She once said that 'were it not for my Archbishop of Canterbury, I should be off in my plane to Longchamps every Sunday.' In spite of the intrusive glare of the modern media, the Queen has been able to enjoy a happy and to a surprising extent, private, family life. When she was twenty-one she married a distant cousin, Philip Mountbatten, whom she first met when she was thirteen. He has proved a popular if outspoken consort, and like Queen Victoria's Albert has created a positive role for himself alongside the Queen. They have three sons and a daughter who have all been to boarding schools and so avoided the enclosed, hot-house atmosphere which up to now has been usual for royal children tutored at home.

The winds of change that Harold Macmillan referred to in the 1960s may have blown strongly in the twenty-five years of Elizabeth's reign, but the monarchy itself has maintained a fairly stable profile. Women's hems may rise or fall but the Queen herself manages to appear timeless without looking ridiculous. During recent years the Queen has drawn closer to her subjects through such means as television and the 'walk-about', during which she can stop and chat at random to bystanders. The Silver Jubilee year of the Queen's accession to the throne resulted almost in a cult of monarchy, with royal souvenirs of every description, Jubilee street parties and a marathon Commonwealth and British tour by the Queen and Prince Philip. Colour television has enabled more people than ever before to share in the pageantry and glamour surrounding the throne. Elsewhere presidents may come and go but the British monarchy looks as if it could endure for ever.

PREVIOUS PAGE *Painting by Pietro Annigoni, Worshipful Company of Fishmongers*

Charles, Prince of Wales

The eldest son of Queen Elizabeth and the Duke of Edinburgh, Prince Charles was born on 14 November 1948, heir to the throne. He was invested Prince of Wales in June 1969.

Selected Index of Personages